Contents

Before You Begin

Before you get started learning, here are some tips to help you become the best guitarist you can be:

1. Don't overwhelm yourself! Pace your learning and practice everything that's taught
2. Don't skip around or put off learning something just because you don't find it interesting, we *all* have to learn the chords and scales when starting to play
3. Get yourself a metronome (they keep time) and a tuner (even if it's just a mobile application, just make sure it employs your microphone)
4. Practice every day for at least 30 minutes and make sure to learn to play the songs you enjoy listening to (otherwise technique and theory work can be very boring!)
5. Have fun no matter what you're doing

When you're stuck playing through your scales every day, make sure to keep number five in mind, whether you're learning a song or changing your strings, having fun is the most important thing of all!

Guitar Basics

Parts of the Guitar

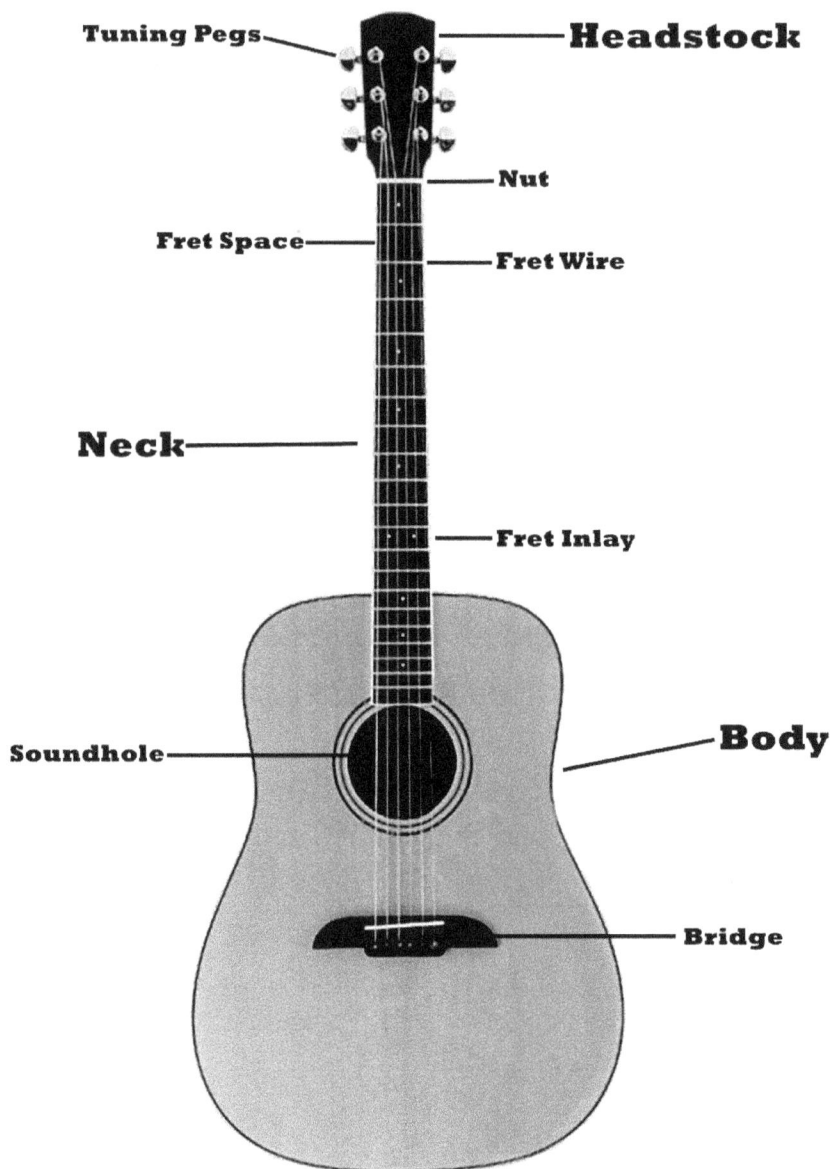

Tuning Pegs — **Headstock**

— Nut

Fret Space — — Fret Wire

Neck —

— Fret Inlay

Soundhole — — **Body**

— Bridge

On the headstock, you'll find six tuning pegs that you can use to tighten and loosen the strings. On the neck, you'll find metal fret wires which separate the fret spaces. Certain frets (namely the 1st, 3rd, 5th, etc.) may have inlays or fret markers that help you quickly see which fret you're playing in (they'll likely be dots, trapezoids, or another shape). The front side of the neck where you'll find the frets and inlays is called the finger or fretboard. Right where the headstock meets the fingerboard, you'll see a nut. The nut has six slots, one for each string, to keep them properly aligned as they go down the neck to where they connect at the bridge. You'll also find a string saddle on the bridge to help align them as well. The shape and size of your guitar, along with the type of wood it is made from, will all affect the tone of your guitar.

Finger Numbers

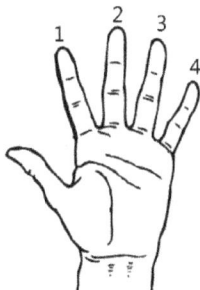

When playing guitar, your fretting hand fingers each get a number. You're fretting hand will be the opposite of your writing hand, so if you're right-handed use your left, and if you're left-handed use your right. We're going to assume you're right handed and will be fretting notes with your left-hand. Your pointer finger is 1, your middle finger 2, your ring finger 3, and your small finger is 4. Your thumb won't get a number because you won't be using it to fret any strings.

String Names

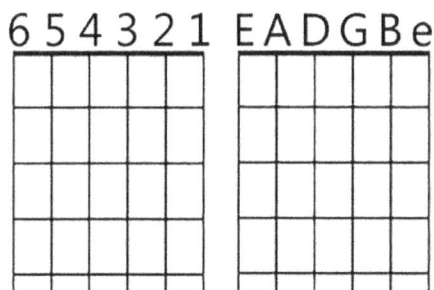

The strings on your guitar may be referred to in multiple ways, the simplest being by number. The thickest string (the one that should be closest to your chin when holding your guitar) is number 6 and the thinnest string (closest to the floor) is number 1. You can also refer to the strings by the note they are tuned to when in standard tuning. We'll get your guitar in-tune momentarily, but have a look at the note names in the diagram.

Since both the top and bottom string are tuned to an E note, we have a different way to refer to these two. The thickest E is called the "low E" which is referring to pitch, not position (make sure to remember that) and the high e is your thinnest string.

Chord Frames

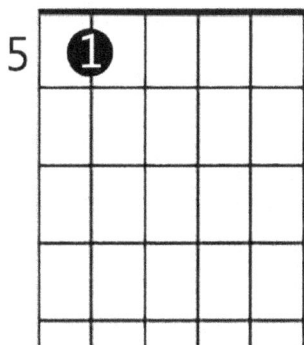

Chord frames show a snapshot of the neck of your guitar and tell you how to play a chord. When standing up straight (vertical), it's like you have your guitar standing up in front of you and you're looking at the neck, so the thickest string is on the left and the thinnest string is on the right. They can also be on their side, if that's the case, it's like someone is holding your guitar the wrong way horizontally, so the thickest string is on the bottom and the thinnest is on top. If there is a number shown next to a space, that's telling you what fret you should be playing in, looking at the diagram, you can see we're in the 5th fret. The dots tell you what strings to hold down on which fret and the numbers on the dots (which won't always be there) tell you which fingers to use.

Notice that it's telling you to use your first finger to hold down the A (5th) string on the 5th fret. If you ever see an "X" on top of a string, don't play it. An "O" means play the string open.

Getting in Tune

Getting your guitar into standard tuning is essential if you want to sound good when you play. Save yourself the trouble of hours' worth of frustration and get yourself a clip-on tuner. They go right on your headstock and will get you in tune within a few minutes. If that's not an option, you can use a method called "relative tuning" or the fifth fret method. It's important to note that this method tunes all of your strings in relation to your low E string so if that string's not already in tune you're not going to end up in standard tuning, but you'll still sound alright.

Fifth Fret Method

1. Hold your low E string down on the 5th fret and play the A string open (without holding it down). Turn the tuning peg of the A string until you can play both strings simultaneously and the pitches match. When the strings are played together, listen for beats. The shorter the "pulses" the more out-of-tune the string is. To raise the pitch, tighten the string, to lower the pitch, loosen it.
2. Next, hold your A string down on the 5th fret and play the D open. Tune the D string until they match in pitch.
3. After that, hold your D string down on the 5th fret and tune the open G to that note.
4. Now, hold the G down on the **4th** fret and tune the open B string to that note.
5. Lastly, hold the B on the 5th fret and tune the high e string to that same note.

As you can see, this method can be a little time consuming if you're completely out of tune, but it's good to memorize in case it's ever your only option. This is also an easy way to make sure you're in tune before practicing. Using your ears is very important to playing well on guitar!

If you happen to have a piano or keyboard lying around, here are the notes to use:

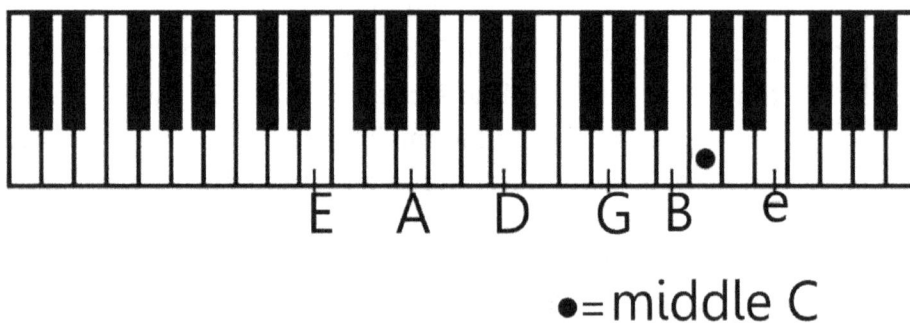

E A D G B e

•=middle C

Get in the habit of checking to make sure you're in tune each time before you play. If you find your guitar going out of tune frequently, stretch your strings. Newer strings have to stretch to length before they'll keep their tuning. Stretch them by grabbing them and pulling them outwards from the body. You should also always tune *up* to a note, instead of down. So, don't tune from an F to an E, tune from a D to an E (upwards in pitch).

Holding Your Guitar

When practicing, you can choose to either sit or stand. Sitting will probably be your choice. If so, use an armless chair so you have plenty of room to move. You may also want to use a foot stool to bring your feet to a comfortable height. When sitting, rest the body of your guitar on the leg that's on the same side as your strumming hand. When standing, always use a strap. Your guitar should be at about the same height standing up as it was when you were sitting down. Keep the neck slightly elevated for ease of playing. Whether sitting or standing, you shouldn't have to support the neck at all with your hands, the strap and the way you're positioned should support the guitar for you.

Hand Positioning

Your fretting hand should be resting around the guitar neck, not gripping it. Holding it with any amount of tension or force will really inhibit your abilities when you start to play. Instead, just lightly rest your hand around the neck, making sure to keep your wrist nearly straight. Bent wrists can lead to injury, so adjust your shoulder and drop your elbow nearer to the floor in order to straighten your forearm. The thumb of your fretting hand should be on the back of the neck and positioned so it's either in between your first and middle finger or in between your middle and third finger. Don't hug your elbow to your side; keep your arm and hand relaxed.

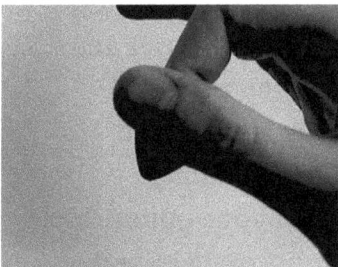

Your strumming hand's arm should be slightly bent at the elbow and resting on the edge of the guitar body. Your pick should be in between your first finger and thumb. Hold onto it just enough so it doesn't fall out of your hand. The pointed tip should appear as though it's coming out of the side of your thumb. Don't use more than these two fingers to grip the pick.

Fretting Notes

To hold down or fret a note on your guitar, you need to place one of your fingers on the string, right behind the fret wire. Don't get too close, that will cause the string to buzz when you play it. Don't press too hard either, just enough so the string rings out clearly. You'll probably find that fretting notes hurts your fingers at first, but soon enough you'll get calluses to protect your fingertips.

Make sure your fingers are arched slightly, not flat. You want to fret notes with your fingertips and you don't want your fingers touching other strings and unintentionally muting them. If only some of your fingers hurt, make sure you're using all four of them evenly. A lot of players avoid using their 4th finger because it tends to be weak, but only playing with three fingers will hinder your speed, technique, and ability.

9

Strumming & Picking Technique

There are two strumming hand techniques to use: floating and resting. Resting is when your wrist is propped on the bridge (behind the saddles) of your guitar so you can pick strings easily. It helps keep your hand steady so you can make small, but quick wrist movements. Make sure you aren't muting the strings; all notes should ring out clearly. The other position, floating, is best for strumming. Trying to strum when your wrist is resting on the bridge is hard. To strum, remove your wrist and rest your forearm on the edge of the body to help you make large movements.

When picking strings, always alternate your picking, getting into the bad habit of only down picking will limit your speed and ability. Whether you're playing scales or practicing a song, always alternate your picking.

Strumming shouldn't always be alternated like picking, but you should practice both down and up strums. The strumming pattern of a song will determine how many times and in which direction you should strum a chord. If you're simply practicing chords on your own and not in the context of a song just alternate you're strumming with down-up-down-up. You always want to start on a down strum when possible. To get your strumming technique correct, you want the motion to be similar to a flicking motion. Act as though there's water on your fingertips and you're flicking it off. That's just about how relaxed your wrist should be. Your forearm should be controlling the movements.

Pick Sizes & Materials

The pick you choose can have a great effect on your tone and playing abilities. Don't get a super-thick pick if you're going to be doing a lot of strumming. Likewise, don't get an extremely thin pick if you're planning on soloing a lot. The thickness of the pick will determine both its flexibility and durability. Picks that are more flexible tend to suit strumming better, while those that don't bend too much will be better for picking individual notes quickly. The material of the pick can change the tone of your guitar. Most are celluloid, while others are acrylic and ceramic. The material you choose is based entirely on preference.

Celluloid picks go dull after being used for a while, but they can be sharpened by rubbing the edge of them against carpet. Acrylic picks are durable, but usually are thicker and less flexible; when they go dull, you'll normally have to replace them or attempt to sharpen them with an emery board. Other materials have their advantages and disadvantages, too.

The size and shape of the pick will affect your technique when playing. Most picks you'll find will be celluloid and shaped like a teardrop. Jazz style picks are very thick and smaller in size and shape. There are endless amounts to choose from, take the time to try out different picks to see what you like best. If you can't seem to find one you like, many famous guitarists use coins (most notably Brian May from Queen).

Reading Tablature

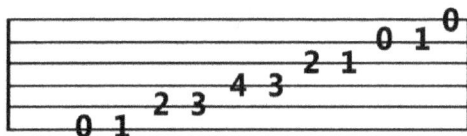

```
|_____0‾|
|_____0__1_____|
|_____2__1_____|
|_____4_3_____|
|_____2__3_____|
|__0__1_____|
```

Guitar tablature, or "tabs," is specific to the instrument. They show 6 horizontal lines, each one representing a string. The thickest, low E string is on the bottom, and the thinnest, high e string is on the top (just like horizontal chord frames). On these lines, you'll see numbers which represent frets. There are no indicators for finger numbers in tab. In the example diagram, you can see that we start on the low E string, and then play up until we reach the high e string. Even though the tablature doesn't tell us which fingers to use, we should know that we can and should use more than one to play all of these notes. That's when the one-fret-per-finger rule comes into play. While it doesn't always apply, a good rule to follow is to give each finger a fret to play in. It'd make since in this example to give our first finger the first fret, second finger the second fret, and so forth. This allows us to play the piece quickly and easily and builds up our dexterity. If you ever see notes stacked on top of one-another it means play them at the same time.

You're probably not going to see many tabs that are only numbers. Acoustic guitar has dozens of techniques to give you different sounds, and since guitar tabs are so common, people have come up with many different ways to notate these techniques when writing out songs. Here are some common signs you may see in tablature:

Symbol	Description	Examples
~~	Shown behind a note, it means apply vibrato	8~~
W~~	"Wide Vibrato"	8w~~
^	Bend the note upwards	8^
F.B.	"Full bend" meaning bend up a whole-step	8 F.B.
R.	Release the bend (bring it back down)	8r
H.	Hammer-on to the note	8h9
P.	Pull-off to the note	8p7
/	Slide up to the note	8/9 or /12
\	Slide down to the note	8/7 or \5

Tablature has no universal notation legend, so every writer invents their own signs to tell you how to play certain notes. This, and the fact that tablature has no real rhythmic notation are the two main downfalls of guitar tablature.

Practicing

Make sure to practice each day, for at least 30 to 45 minutes. Always review what you've learned and make sure to practice songs along with technique and theory. Knowing how to apply what you learn is essential to becoming a great guitarist. Take plenty of time with each lesson and make sure to really practice and understand everything before moving on. Rushing through these lessons or anything else when learning guitar won't get you very far and will likely just end up making you frustrated.

The Musical Alphabet

The seven natural notes in the musical alphabet are: A-B-C-D-E-F-G which repeat again and again. There is no "H" note in western music. In between the natural notes are something called accidentals, or sharps and flats. A sharp note is 1 half-step higher than a natural note, while a flat note is 1 half-step lower. On the guitar, 1 half-step is equal to 1 fret. It's easiest to count the fret wire in this case. Shown in the diagram is the musical alphabet, with sharps and flats included.

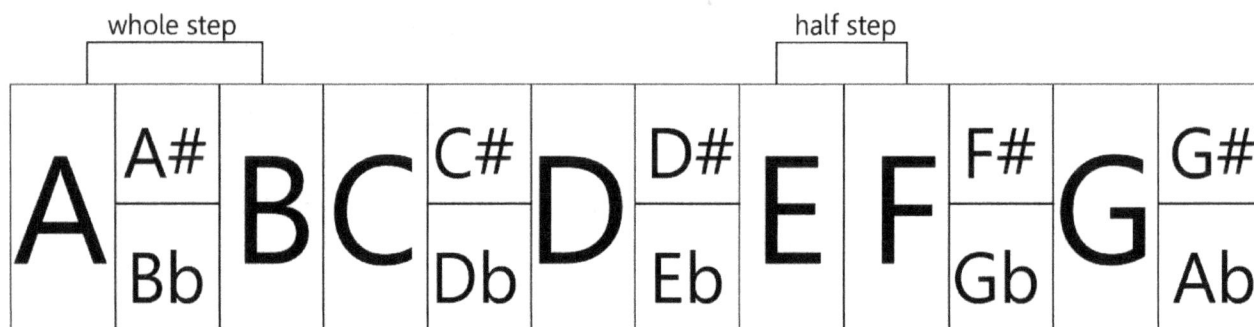

The notes that are stacked on top of one another, like A# and Bb are called "enharmonic equivalents" which simply means they're the same note, but with different names for theoretical purposes. So, if you play the first fret of the A string, you'll be playing an A# or Bb, depending on what you wish to call it. They sound the same, and they're played the same, but they have two different names for theory's sake. Since these notes are the same, you don't have to include both sharps and flats when writing the musical alphabet, in fact, you'll most likely see it written with only sharps, like so: A-A#-B-C-C#-D-D#-E-F-F#-G-G#.

As you may have guessed, two half-steps equal one whole-step. Since one half-step is equal to one fret (wire), a whole-step, or two half-steps, will be equal to two fret wires on the guitar. All natural notes in the musical alphabet are a whole-step (two fret wires) apart, with two exceptions: B and C are a half-step apart, and E and F are a half-step apart. Looking back at the diagram, you can see there is nothing in between these notes. That's because B#/Cb and E#/Fb cannot be played on your guitar.

Theoretical Notes

Even though B#, Cb, E# and Fb cannot be played on your guitar, they do exist within written music. Once you begin to learn guitar and music theory, you'll likely see one of these four notes written down somewhere, whether it is within a key chart, song, or scale diagram. Even though an F will be played where E# is written, and a C will be played where B# is written, writing in what will be played instead of what's actually part of the piece would be theoretically incorrect. So, if you ever happen to be working out a scale or interval of any kind and there happens to be a Cb included, don't write in a C note just because that's the note you'll end up playing, write in the note that's correct in theory.

Notes on the Neck

Once you know the musical alphabet, you should start to memorize the location of all the notes on the neck of your guitar. Here's a quick-reference diagram:

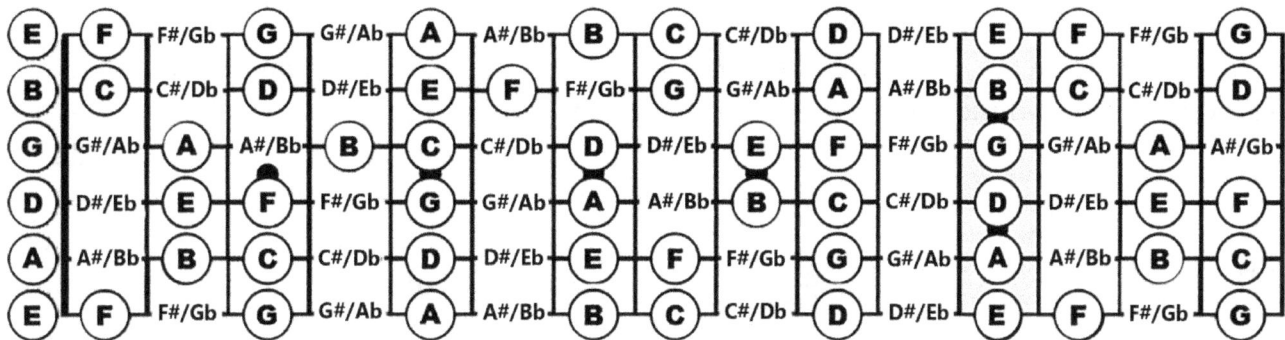

E	F	F#/Gb	G	G#/Ab	A	A#/Bb	B	C	C#/Db	D	D#/Eb	E	F	F#/Gb	G
B	C	C#/Db	D	D#/Eb	E	F	F#/Gb	G	G#/Ab	A	A#/Bb	B	C	C#/Db	D
G	G#/Ab	A	A#/Bb	B	C	C#/Db	D	D#/Eb	E	F	F#/Gb	G	G#/Ab	A	A#/Gb
D	D#/Eb	E	F	F#/Gb	G	G#/Ab	A	A#/Bb	B	C	C#/Db	D	D#/Eb	E	F
A	A#/Bb	B	C	C#/Db	D	D#/Eb	E	F	F#/Gb	G	G#/Ab	A	A#/Bb	B	C
E	F	F#/Gb	G	G#/Ab	A	A#/Bb	B	C	C#/Db	D	D#/Eb	E	F	F#/Gb	G

As you can see, you start on the open string note then simply go up through the musical alphabet from there. At the 12th fret, everything repeats again. That's because there's only 12 notes in the musical alphabet: A-A#-B-C-C#-D-D#-E-F-F#-G-G#, each 1 half-step, or 1 fret apart. You can think of the nut as a fret wire in this situation.

Some important notes to remember as reference points would be those on the low E and A strings. Most people remember the third fret notes of these strings with the saying "3 Great Cats" G being the low E string note and C being the A string note at the third fret. On the fifth fret, you can use "5 Able Digits" A being the low E note and D being the A string note. For the 7th fret, "7 Beautiful Elephants" works well to remind you the low E note is B and the A string note is E. Since you know C always follows B and F always follows E, you'll also have the 8th fret notes of these two strings memorized.

Since the 12th fret notes are the same as the open string notes, you can bar that fret with your finger (hold down all the strings at once) and act as though your finger is the guitar nut. Now the 13th fret can be seen as the 1st fret, the 14th the second, and so on. To find the "matching" fret of a note above the 12th fret, just take the fret number and subtract 12. So, the 17th fret notes are the same as the (17-12) 5th fret notes. The inlays may also match up on your guitar neck.

If you ever hear tones being used instead of steps, you should know that 1 semitone is equal to 1 half-step, and 1 whole tone is the same as 1 whole-step. Tones are used primarily in England while steps are the standard for America.

Each week, pick a note and practice each day locating it across the neck to help you remember it. You can also look for patterns across the fretboard to help you remember. For example, many people use a "W" shape as reference across the fretboard. If you circle all of the F notes on the fretboard, then connect them, you'll find it, too (it will work with any and all notes, but F is a good place to start).

Musical Notation

Musical notation tends to appear slightly intimidating at first, but it's actually quite simple to understand once you can see everything that's going so.

Note Appearance & Measures

First, let's focus on the notes you're seeing. The lines ("stems") connected to the noteheads can point in either direction and have no effect on the duration or pitch of the note, they're simply put in place for ease of reading, and they may be omitted on occasion. The small piece of staff you see in the diagram is known as a measure. Pieces of music are broken down into measures to make counting rhythms much easier. Measures are separated by vertical lines on the staff, like so:

A single barline separates measures, a double barline typically ends a section of the piece, and a terminal barline ends the song. Measures are also called "bars."

Clefs & Time Signatures

Going back to the first piece of staff seen, you may notice the clef sign (the fancy "G"). This is known as the treble clef, all guitar music is represented with this clef. The fraction beside the clef sign is known as the time signature. It tells you how many beats are in a measure, and which type of note is worth one beat. In 4/4 or common time, there are four beats per measure, and a quarter note (1/4) gets 1 beat. The BPM (beats per minute) is represented with the number above the staff. In this case, there are 120 BPM (measured in quarter notes).

Accidentals & Notes on the Staff

The first line on the staff (on the bottom) is an E note. All the notes go in alphabetical order from bottom to top, so after E is F (bottom space), then G (second line), then A (second space), and so on. The spaces spell "FACE" and the line that the end of the clef sign wraps around is always a G note (hence why it's also called the G clef). Only natural notes appear on the staff unless a key signature is shown (more on that in a minute), but if there's a piece of music that happens to have a sharp or flat temporarily, you'll see a sign on the staff noting that. It will always be placed before the notehead on the staff. These signs will last for the remainder of the measure unless canceled out again by a natural sign (last sign shown).

14

Ledger Lines

Ledger lines temporarily extend the staff for notes that won't fit. Keep in mind that the lower the notes are placed on the staff, the lower they are in pitch when played. Shown are the open string notes.

Key Signatures

You're likely to encounter a piece of staff with sharps or flats next to the clef sign. The

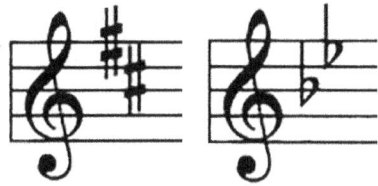

sharps and flats are showing you the key signature, which simply means which notes are supposed to be sharped or flatted in the piece. Instead of drawing in an accidental (sharp, flat, natural) sign beside every note that should be sharped or flatted in the song, we use key signatures to denote it ahead of time. The space or line on which the signs are placed show you which notes should be raised or lowered. In the above key signatures, C and F are supposed to be sharped. In the second key signature, B and E are supposed to be flatted.

Looking again at the key signature containing sharps, we know that whenever we see a C or F note, we should play it as a C# or F#. So, even though the notes are written where a C or F natural note would normally be, the key signature is

telling us to play them all as C# and F#. It would be in these cases when the natural sign is used. Even though the key signature is telling us to play all occurrences of these two notes sharped, we may need to have a natural note, too. This is the time when you would place a natural sign before whichever note should be played natural. This cancellation will last for the remainder of the measure, but it will only apply to the single octave is was placed in. For example, if we only placed the natural note next to middle C (on the ledger line), the C note found in the third space would still be played as C#.

The second and first measures are identical, but as you can see, it takes up a lot more space to write the sharps in next to each note. If you ever add in accidental signs that aren't part of the key signature, keep in mind that they will only last for the rest of the measure and that they only apply to the octave they were written in (just like natural signs).

Note & Rest Durations

whole   half   quarter   eighth   sixteenth

Here's a breakdown of the most common note durations. A whole note lasts 4 beats, a half note 2 beats, quarter 1 beat, eighth ½ beat, and a sixteenth ¼ beat.

whole   half   quarter   eighth   sixteenth

Rests are used to tell how long you should wait to play the next note. Just like their note counterparts, whole rests last 4 beats, half rests last 2 beats, quarter rests last 1, eighth ½, and sixteenth rests ¼ beat.

Beamed & Dotted Notes

Notes are frequently beamed together when they last for less than 1 beat. Beams do not change the duration of the note, they just help make them easier to read. The first set is eighth notes; we know this because there's only 1 beam connecting them (just like there's only one flag on individual eighth notes and rests). The second set are sixteenth notes, notice the double beam connecting the four notes.

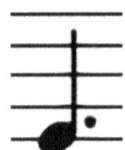

Dotted notes are equal to the normal duration, plus half of it (or the note x1.5 in length). A dotted quarter note, for instance, is worth a 1/4+1/8 beat. Just hold the note for that amount of time, there's no need to play it twice or anything.

Chords

To show chords on the staff, there may be stacked notes or actual chord names written above the staff with rhythm slashes (hash marks) below them.

Looking at the rhythm slashes, you can see eighth notes still have one flag while sixteenth notes have two. You can also beam these notes together, just like regular notes.

16

Counting Rhythms

Typically, you can count: 1-and-2-and-3-and-4-and when playing in 4/4 time. Here's how this goes with the following note durations:

Quarter notes each get 1 beat in 4/4 time. In this measure, we're playing them on the down beat (the numbers) and are letting them last throughout the upbeats (the "ands")

Eighth notes are played twice as fast as quarter notes because they last half as long. In this measure, we are playing eighth notes on both the downbeats and upbeats.

Sixteenth notes are counted as follows:

Spoken "1 e and uh," this method can get very slurred at quick tempos so a system known as "Takadimi" is used as an alternative. Here's how that looks with sixteenth notes:

Taking the time to learn how to count rhythms now will save you countless hours of trouble in the future. Knowing how to play even the simplest of rhythms (and practicing them) will help you build your speed and overall playing abilities.

Pickup Rhythms

Pickup rhythms are measures that start on a beat other than one. For example, instead of showing rests signs at the beginning of a measure, they could be omitted all together and just the notes that will be played are written.

Say you have a song in 4/4 time but it starts on beat 4, instead of beginning the song with rests, you can make it a pickup rhythm and put only a single note in the first measure. You'd count in "1-2-3" then start playing on "4."

Sight-Reading

Practicing your sight-reading abilities is extremely important. It's a skill you always have to work on and one you risk losing if you quit practicing. Use a metronome and set it at a slow tempo to start. Make sure you pay attention to the note durations and pitches shown. Most importantly, read a couple notes ahead as you play. Take advantage of the long-lasting notes to quickly familiarize yourself with the measure.

Twinkle, Twinkle Little Star

The numbers, like "5" and "9" are telling you which measure you're looking at. 4/4 time is also called common time and may be represented with a "c" in some cases. If you see a "C" with a line splitting it down the middle, it means half of 4/4 time (2/2 time). If you ever see "8va" written it's telling you to play the notes an octave higher than written. An octave is a kind of interval and is made up of 8 whole-steps or 12 half-steps. If you play an open G, then play it on the 12th fret, you'll be playing it 1 octave higher than the open note. All 12th fret notes are 1 octave higher than their corresponding open string note.

The double dots by the barline are telling you to repeat everything in between. If there's only one repeat sign, repeat from the beginning.

Songs like this one are great for increasing your ability to sight-read, but you should also practice ones that include chords, different time signatures, and other key signatures. Always use a metronome when playing any piece of music, especially when it's in the form of musical notation.

Review the note durations and rest signs frequently to keep your memory sharp. Taking a piece of sheet music and putting it into another key is a great way to learn the different pitches and memorize all of the durations and key signatures.

High e Jams

All of these notes are found on the high e string within the first few frets.

Notice that the previous terminal barline means this is another piece:

The below riff uses eighth notes, ties, rhythm dots and rests:

Remember 1 beam means it's a set of eighth notes. The rest signs can be found on page 16. Tied notes should only be played once, so in measure five only pick the F note one time, but let its duration last for the length of two quarter notes (1 half note). Recall the rhythm dot makes a note last 1.5 times its normal length, so let the quarter note last for the length of a quarter and eighth note.

Even though all of these notes can be found on a single string, exercises like this allow you to focus on the durations and signs rather than where the next note will be. They also help you memorize these first-position notes slowly. The following pages will have riffs like these to help you with first-position notes on all of the strings. In case you didn't know, first-position simply means that it's played within the first few frets on the neck.

19

B String Jams

Here are the first-position notes on the B string:

Here's a practice piece that incorporates rests, dots, and sixteenth notes, take it slow at first, we recommend no more than 60 beats per minute for this one:

If you need help with these rhythms, page 17 has the counting examples. Make sure you practice until you get them right, don't put it off to learn another time, do it now so you'll know how in the future. Here's another first-position riff on the B string:

These riffs might be easy for you, but you should still practice them. Not only are they helping you memorize the first-position notes, count rhythms, and gain speed, they're also increasing your overall dexterity. Make sure you're alternating your picking throughout each piece and that you're counting each note in time with the metronome. The metronome's tempo (BPM) should be set to however fast you want to play quarter notes. So, if you want to play 60 quarter notes per minute that's how fast the metronomes tempo should be (60 BPM). Tap your foot in time to help you keep track.

G String Jams

Here are the first-position notes on the G string, notice that we also added in the sharp and flat notes that can be found in the first-position on this string:

You can see that in measure 6 we showed the enharmonic equivalents in first-position on this string by telling you to play a G# and Ab then an A# and Bb. This was just to remind you that these two notes are played the same but can be written in two different ways. In normal cases, you'll only see sharp notes or flat notes used in a piece, not both (especially not in the same measure with the same notes). Remember that sharps and flats remain for the entire measure unless a natural sign cancels them out early (so have another look at how you may have played measure 8).

Here's one last piece using only the natural notes in first position on the G string:

Remember these riffs aren't really meant to entertain you, just teach you the notes, rhythms, and signs. You should learn songs you enjoy listening to so you don't get bored with all of this technique and theory.

D String Jams

The first-position notes on the D string are shown below (we show natural notes only):

Here's a simple jam using these notes:

When first starting to read music you may want to write in one or two of the tough rhythms or notes into a couple of the measures for reference to help you learn, but don't do it with all of the songs, only ones you have a lot of trouble with. If you write in fret or string numbers, only use them if you have to, always read the notes that are written. Fingerings should be used only as a last resort if you're really stuck.

The above rhythm is a little tricky. The first measure has a typical set of eighth notes, but that's followed by 5 notes beamed together. Those 5 notes are a set of 2 sixteenth notes followed by three eighth notes. It probably looks a little more complicated than it is; all you do is count it off if you get stuck. The (entire) first measure is counted: 1 & 2 & (eighth notes) 3 e & 4 & (second set). So, all together: 1 & 2 & 3 e & 4 &. Remember the metronome is clicking on the numbers, or quarter notes, so use them as reference when playing.

A String Jams

The natural A string notes in first-position are:

Notice these notes are lower in pitch so they're all added using ledger lines. C (middle C) is on the first ledger line below the staff, right below it (in the space) is B then A is on the second line. Here's another practice piece:

Recall eighth note rests have one flag (see the third measure). The first measure has sixteenth, eighth, and quarter notes, so let's have a brief look at counting this piece.

In measure one, we start with 1 e & 2 & 3 & 4 &. Let's break that down, we have the "1 e" on the pair of sixteenth notes, then the "& 2" for the eighth notes that follow. Next, the first quarter note falls on the "& 3," the second quarter note is on "& 4" and the final eighth note is on the "&." Measure two is quite simple with quarter notes and rests, just 1 & 2 & 3 & 4 & (one number for each quarter note/rest). We would just play the quarter notes on each metronome click. In measure 3, you'd count 1 & 2 & 3 & 4, where "1 &" is the first quarter note, "2" is the eighth rest, "& 3" is the second quarter note, "& 4" is the third quarter note, and the final eighth rest ends up on the "&". This riff has a lot of playing on the "upbeats" of the song. This basically means if you were strumming this rhythm with chords, you'd be down-strumming on the numbers (the downbeat) and up-strumming on the "&" signs (the upbeat). Rhythms with up-beats can be hard to get the feel for, so practice for a while to get it right.

The remainder of the piece is made up of eighth, quarter and half notes. Take the time to write out these rhythms to make sure you're counting them correctly.

Low E Jams

The low E natural notes are shown below:

Once you have to start adding multiple ledger lines it can be slightly hard to read. As we said before, notes that should be played an octave up are represented by "8va," there's also a sign to show you notes should be played one octave lower, and that's represented with "8vb." You may occasionally see notes on this string (and other strings) written higher on the staff somewhere with this sign.

Here's a final piece to practice before we put all of the first-position notes together, take your time and review these exercises regularly until you can play them quicker and more accurately (without memorizing!):

Practice these single-string pieces until you're comfortable with them before moving on. Gradually speed up the tempo once you can play them slowly, 120 BPM is a good goal.

First-Position Overview

Here are all of the first-position notes. The first set shows sharps while the second piece shows flats; they both show the same notes when played. We start on the low E string notes and go up in pitch across the strings, pay attention to the tablature to make sure you're playing everything correctly.

Same notes, but with flats instead of sharps:

Open-Position Major Chords

Open-position chords use both fretted notes and open strings to make up chords.

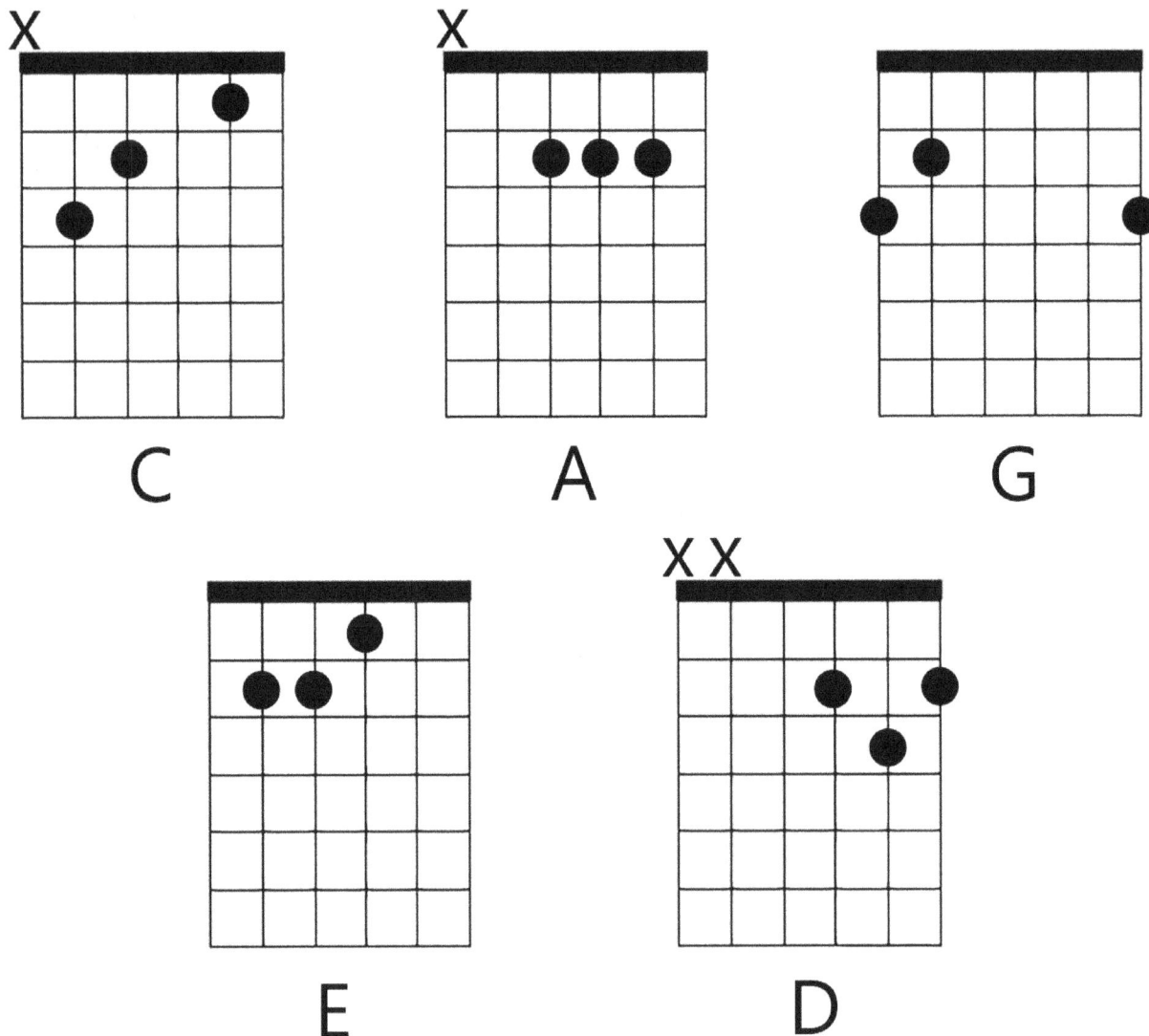

When playing chords, always play from the root note downwards, the root note is what makes the chord what it is. So, the root of the C major chord is the C note, found on the 3rd fret of the A string (so don't play the low E). The root of the A chord is the open A string (again, don't play the low E). In the G and E chords, you should play all of the strings, with the D chord, play from the open D string downwards. Practice playing these chords by strumming them and switching between them.

You may have noticed some notes missing, like B and F. These major chords aren't played in the open-position, so you'll learn them later when we go over bar chords.

Open-Position Major Scales

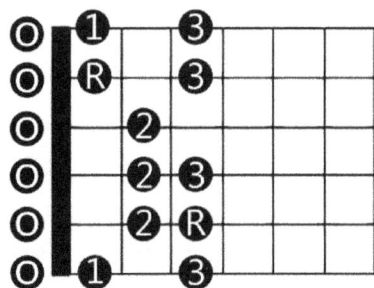
C
(key of C)

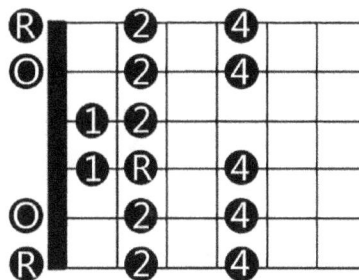
E
(key of E)

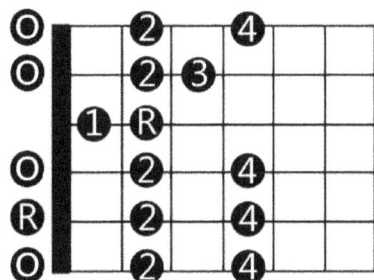
A
(key of A)

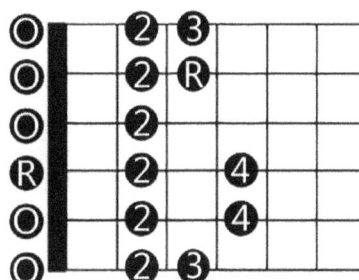
D
(key of D)

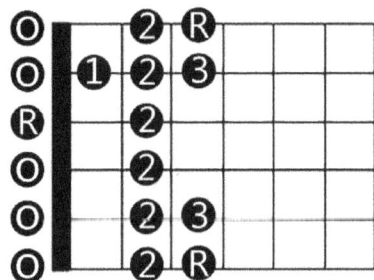
G
(key of G)

A scale is a set of notes; each placed a certain distance apart from one another. If you've ever taken singing lessons, you probably had to warm up with the famous solfège tones: "Do-Re-Me-Fa-Sol-La-Ti-Do" which is the vocal way to sing the major scale, from root (do) to root (do) (the second root being one octave higher than the first). The root, as we briefly mentioned before, is what makes the chord or scale what it is. In other words, if you're playing in the key of C major, your root note in the scale is going to be C. These scale shapes above are each in the key corresponding to their shape name (for example, the D shape is in the key of D major). This doesn't always have to be the case, if you want to change the key, you can take any of the shapes and move the scale so all of the root notes are in whichever key you want to play in. We'll talk more about this in a minute. For now, let's play through our scales. The numbers on the dots are showing you which fingers to use. Changing the fingering won't necessarily make it wrong, but you should get in the habit of using these fingerings. The "R" is showing you where the root notes of the scale are located; make sure to memorize their locations within the scales.

27

Practicing

When playing scales, always start from the lowest (in pitch) root note and play all the way up until the very last note, then play it backwards to the very first note (before the root you started on), then back up to the root note you began with (it's most important to remember that you should always start on the lowest root and end on the lowest root).

If we were to play our G major scale, we'd start on our first root found on the 3rd fret of the low E. We'd play up until the very last note in the scale, which happens to be another root found on the 3rd fret, this time on the high e. Finally, we'd play backwards through our scale, back all the way down to our very first note, the open low E string, then end the scale by playing back up to where we started (the 3rd fret of the low E). Remember to alternate your picking when playing scales.

Play both your scales and chords every day. You want to have these memorized, as they're the basis for all things on guitar.

CAGED System

The scales and chords you learned previously can be moved across the fretboard so you can play in different keys. Before we get into that, let's see how the chords and scales themselves are connected.

Within the C shaped scale, you can find the C major chord (hence why it's called the C shaped scale). Here are the chord notes highlighted in gray.

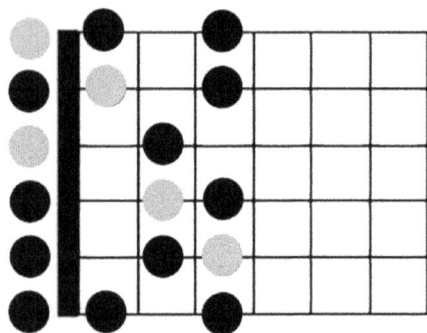

You can find all of the chord shapes in their corresponding scales. Notice how the roots from the scale are included in the chord shape; remember it wouldn't be a C chord unless it had C notes within it.

Now that we know that the chords and scales themselves are connected, we can look at the scale shapes relationships with one another.

First, let's realize that the word "CAGED" is very important. CAGED helps us keep everything in order. You can't rearrange the CAGED system into DACEG. Even though you have to keep these letters in order you can start on any one of them. For instance, you could start on E, which gives you EDCAG (it's still CAGED as long as you go in order) or start on G and get GEDCA.

You can't skip shapes either, so when using the CAGED system always remember: 1) You can start on any letter, but 2) You have to go in order and 3) You cannot skip any letters.

Moveable Shapes

Remember when we were learning the notes on the neck and you used your finger to hold down all the strings on the 12th fret? We're going to do something like that again, but this time we're going to build a chord shape, too! This is what we call bar (or "barre") chords. Basically, you use one finger to hold down multiple strings while your other three build a chord shape.

When you bar the strings, you can think of your finger as the guitar nut, so you can move any open chord shape to anywhere on the neck and have a new chord! If you take one of your open chord shapes right now, you can do this same thing! Let's use G major for instance. Hold down the shape in the open-position, but use only your second, third, and fourth fingers to do it (it may be a little tricky). Now keep holding the shape down, but take your first finger and lay it across the nut, that's what your bar chord shape should look like. Now move the shape so your first finger is barring the first fret (make sure the spacing between your fingers stays the same). That's a G-shaped G# major chord (Notice where your root is: the 4th fret of the low E).

You can do this with any of the chord shapes. The E and A shaped chords are the most common and easiest to get down. If you bar the 7th fret and then build an A shape (keep the spacing correct) you'll have an A-shaped E major chord (the root is on the A-string, remember?). You can also play an E-shaped A major chord by barring the 5th fret and building your E-shape. The bar chord shapes in the key of G major in the order of EDCAG, can be seen on the following page.

If you don't know what a key is yet, it basically tells you what note the root note (or root chord within a song) is placed on. In the following bar chord chart, all of the chord root notes are placed on a G note, meaning they're all different ways to play a G major chord.

Playing Bar Chords

Playing bar chord shapes can be tricky at first. Getting all the right strings to ring out at once without buzzing takes some practice, but that's what you need to do: practice! Spend 15 minutes each day switching between and strumming the bar chords. Move them up and down the neck and play different chords. Here are some tips:

1. Take your time and play each string individually to make sure none of them are unintentionally muted.
2. Don't assume pressing harder will help the notes ring out; this can cause tension issues in the future.
3. Make sure your finger is straight up and down the fret, that you're behind the fret wire, and that no notes are being bent out of place on the neck (press the strings straight onto the fretboard, don't push them up or down).

Major Bar Chord Shapes

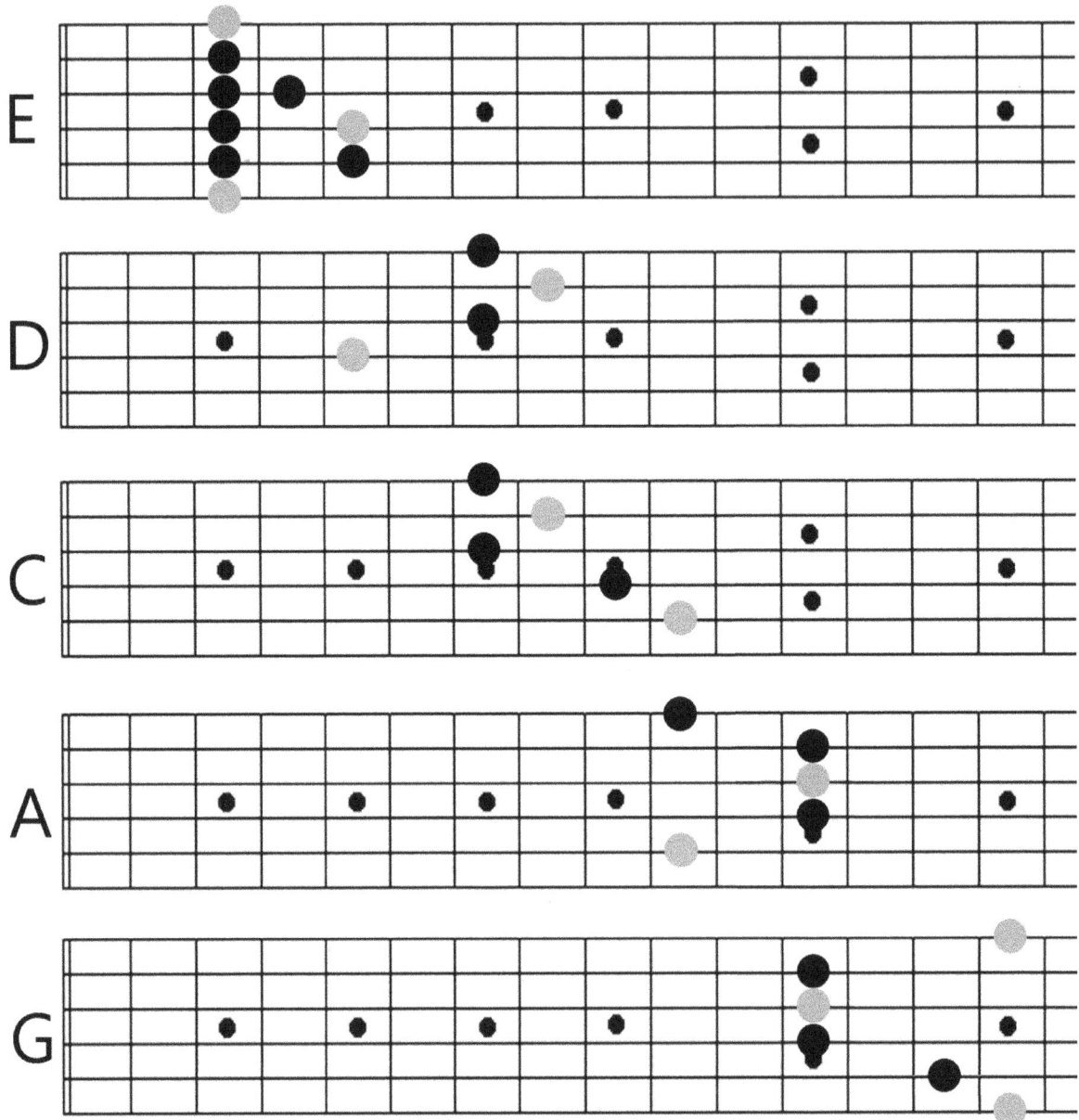

Notice how these shapes aren't getting mixed around. They're going in order through the word "CAGED" starting on the E, then going to D, then C, and so on. As you'll find out, everything on the guitar repeats. We don't have to end after we go through the word CAGED once, we can keep going and going repeatedly (just go in order). After our A shape we can play a G shape again, then another E shape, and a D shape, and on it repeats. Eventually of course, you'll run out of frets.

We can also go backwards through the word CAGED. Before E is G, meaning we can place our open G major chord shape "behind" the E bar chord shape in the above diagram (see how it fits right in?).

Major Scale Shapes

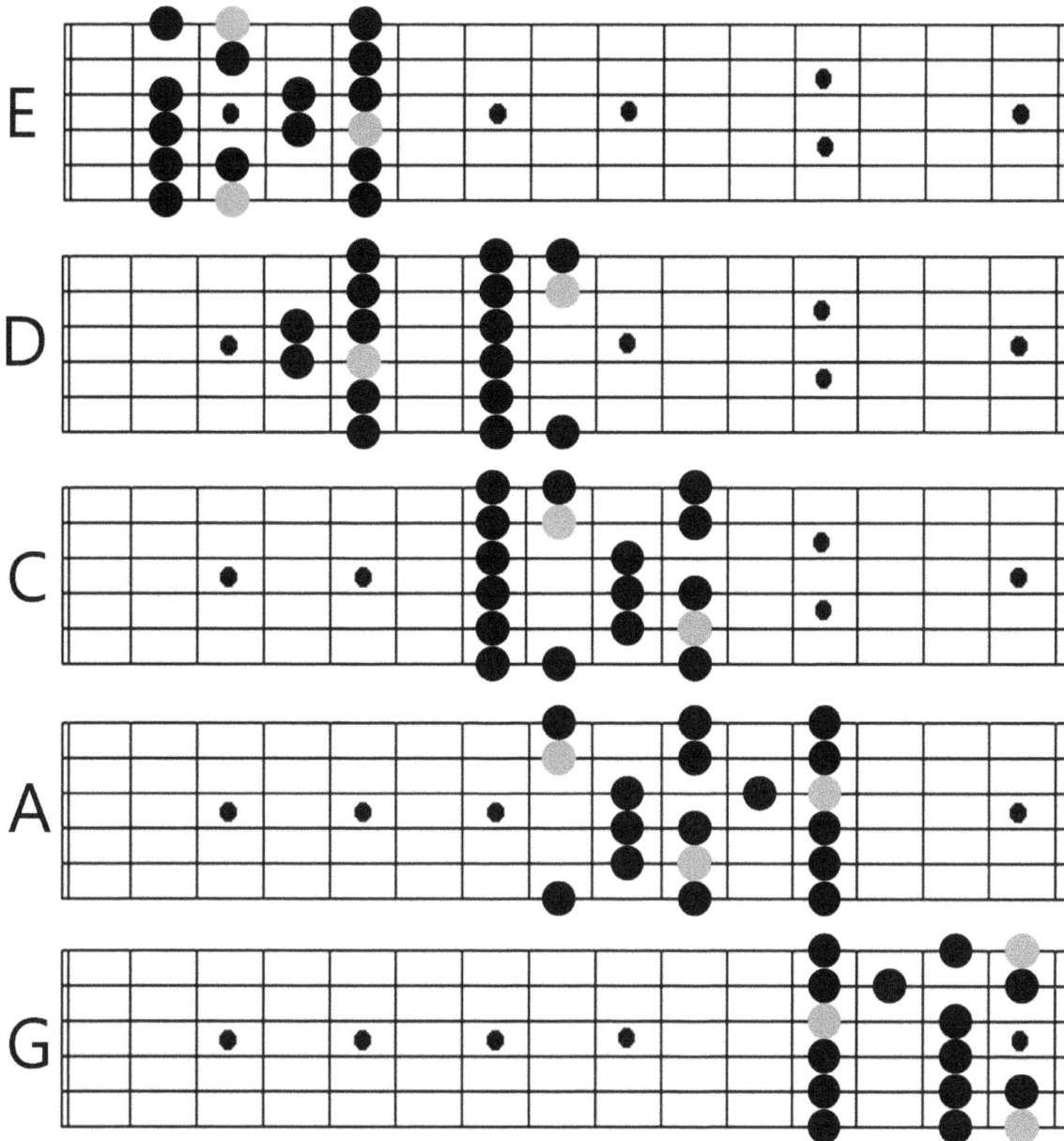

These scale shapes can be a little intimidating when you first see them, but if you've memorized the open-position scale shapes, you've pretty much already got these down. Some of the open-position scale shapes may be slightly different than these, that's because we had to shift some notes so they were in the right key. All we did was take notes from the next consecutive scale and shift the entire scale "backwards" so the root note was in the right place. Practice these scales, and remember to alternate your picking and use all four fingers when playing them. Memorize the location of the root notes (seen in gray) and practice shifting keys. Start on another shape than the E shown here (go in order). Just like with the chords, we can go backwards in the word CAGED and add in the G open-scale shape "behind" the E scale shape. We can also continue adding shapes after the G scale shape on the 15th fret.

31

Major Arpeggio Shapes

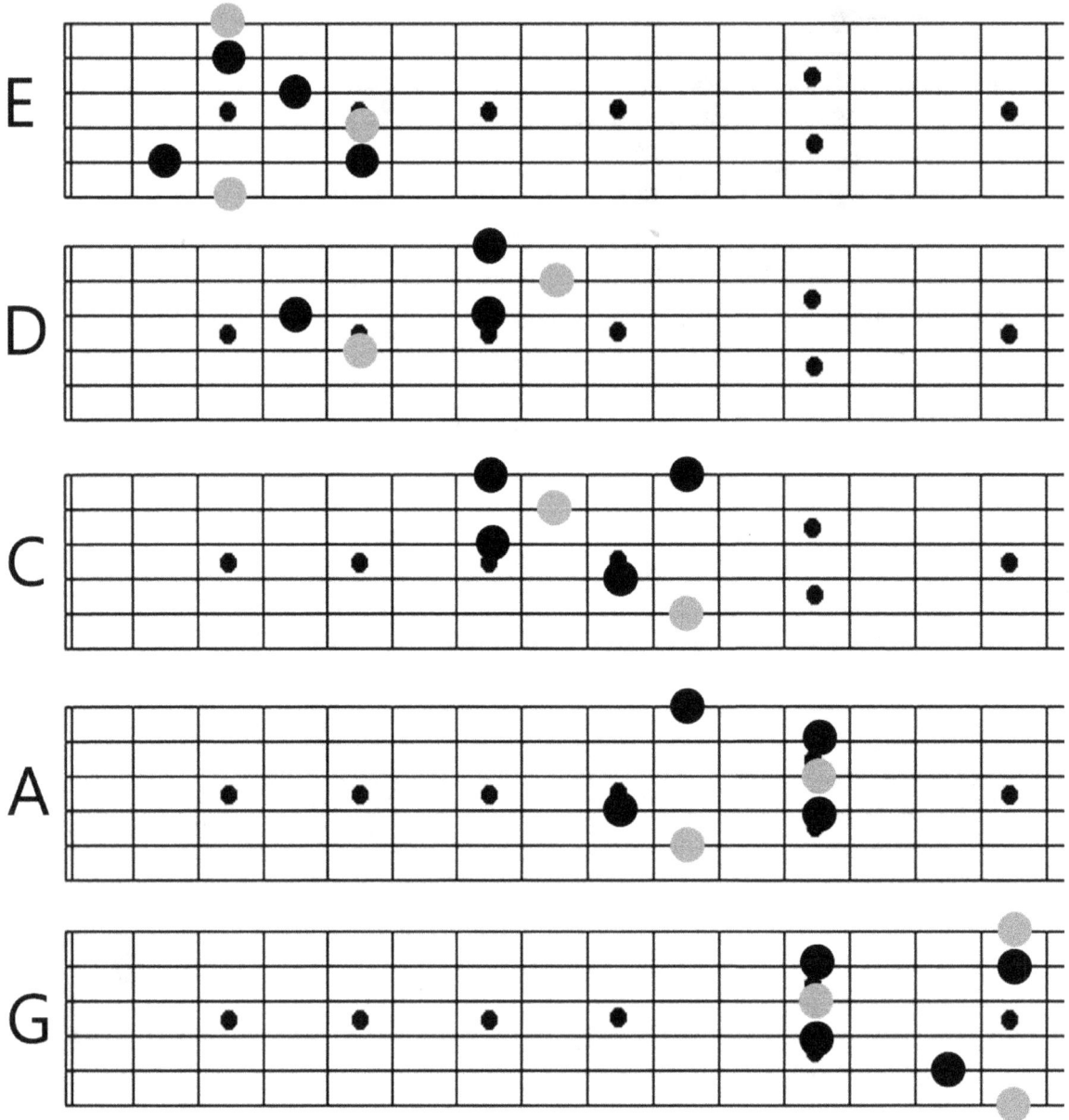

Arpeggios take the 1st, 3rd, and 5th notes of a scale shape. To get the E shape arpeggio, take the E shaped major scale and start with the root as 1, then number each note in order, keeping only the notes numbered 1, 3 or 5. Once you get to the 5, start over again with 1 at the next root note. This is how you build arpeggio shapes. Arpeggios are great for soloing and improvising over chords, so practice using them! They're also great for building dexterity in all of your fingers. Notice how all the root notes and the notes from the corresponding chord shapes remain in the arpeggio shape.

Knowing how to change keys is extremely important. Just memorize the root note locations, keep everything in order, and shift each shape the same amount of frets up or down the neck.

Open-Position Minor Chords

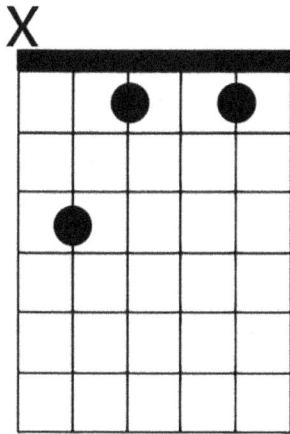

Cm

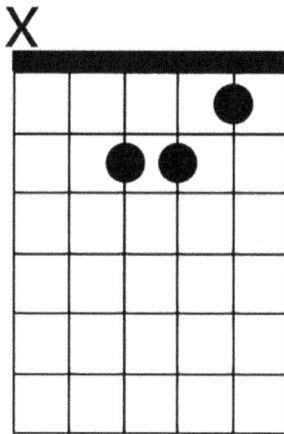

Am

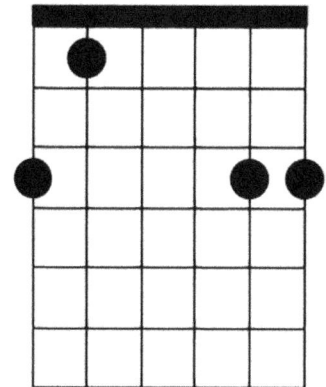

Gm

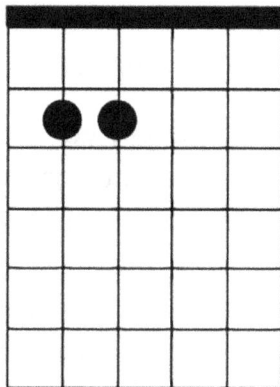

Em

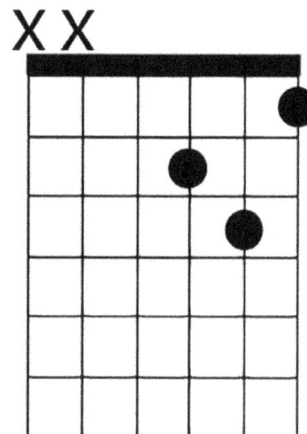

Dm

Notice that major chords are just uppercase letters by themselves, while minor chords usually have a lowercase "m" behind them to let you know it's a minor chord.

Moveable Minor Chords

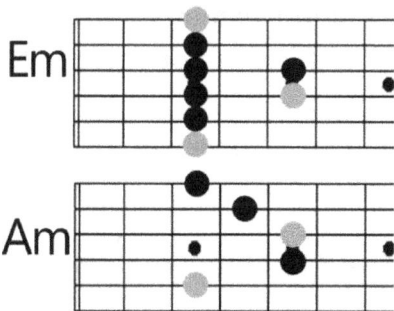

Em

Am

As you may have guessed, there are minor scales and an entire CAGED minor system as well, but we don't really need it right now. Why? Now that you know your open minor chords, we can use those shapes to build all of the major and minor chords that we need. Since we already know how to build chords using the CAGED system, simply by changing root notes, we just need to use some of our minor chord shapes. Pictured are the two most common (and easiest) moveable minor bar chord shapes.

Building Chord Progressions

The shapes you've learned so far were all in the key of G major, so they were all different ways to play G major scales, chords, and arpeggios. You'll obviously want more than one chord if you want to actually play songs, but choosing which chords to use can be a little tricky. Here's a major key chord chart:

Key	I	ii	iii	IV	V	vi	vii
C	C	D	E	F	G	A	B
D	D	E	F#	G	A	B	C#
E	E	F#	G#	A	B	C#	D#
F	F	G	A	Bb	C	D	E
G	G	A	B	C	D	E	F#
A	A	B	C#	D	E	F#	G#
B	B	C#	D#	E	F#	G#	A#

Taking a quick look at the roman numerals at the top of the chart, the uppercase are major and the lowercase are minor, the last box (the 7th) is actually diminished.

Common progressions are I-IV-V and vi-ii-V-I. Take any major key you want to play in, let's say C, and plug in your chords to one of these formulas. Using the chart and the first formula, our I is C major, IV is F major, and our V is G major. You now have a progression in C major: C-F-G. Play them using whichever shapes you like. Make up your own strumming pattern and practice them. Pay attention to whether the chords should be major or minor when building progressions. While it's great to be able to build all the chords on a single string using multiple shapes and positions, you should always try to find the chord closest to your starting position.

Major Key Formula Chart

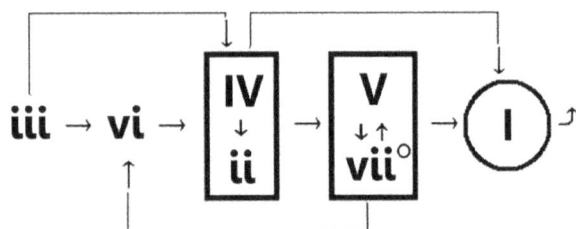

iii → vi → [IV / ii] → [V / vii°] → (I)

This chart shows formulas for chord progressions in any major key. Starting on any number then following the arrows will allow you to put together a song. Remember that lowercase roman numerals are supposed to be played as minor chords, and uppercase are played as major chords. The I chord can be followed by any of the other ones. Note that this shouldn't limit your possibilities. Some progressions may not adhere to these formulas. Always keep in mind: as long as it sounds good it is good, even if theory says otherwise.

Take the time to familiarize yourself with this formula chart and try putting together and playing a few formulas of your own.

Finding I-IV-V Chords

If we start with our C chord on the 8th fret of the low E, where would our closest F major chord be? Right below it on the 8th fret of the A string. Our closest G would be found a whole-step up on the 10th fret of the A string (remember to use the correct shapes for these strings). If we play that same I-IV-V progression in another key, say F, we'll get F-Bb-C. We can put our F major chord on the 1st fret of the low E string, and our closest Bb major chord can be found on the A string on that same fret, just as last time. Just like before, our V chord (C major) can be found a whole-step up on the 3rd fret of the A string.

The pattern is what makes the I-IV-V progression so popular. Going back to the notes on the neck, you may have found many patterns across the fretboard. This is no coincidence, music theory, especially guitar theory, is filled with patterns. The way your guitar is tuned allows for music theory to be easily applied to the guitar.

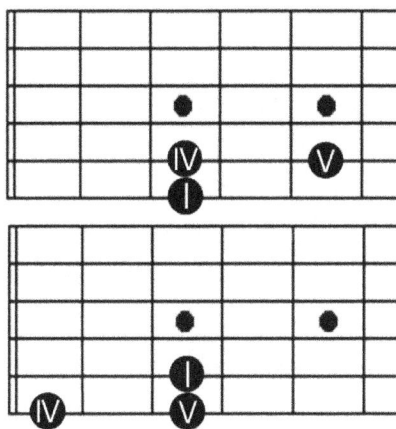

If your I chord is placed on the low E somewhere, you always know your IV chord is going to be directly "below" it on the A string, on that very same fret, and that your V chord will be a whole-step (two fret wires) up towards the body, also on the A string. Put simply in the first diagram, you can see the location of the root notes of each chord (the example is using a G major, G-C-D progression). If you place the root note of your first chord on the A string, you can follow this same pattern, with the IV chord "below" it on the D string, and the V chord a whole-step up. You can also follow another pattern if D shaped chords are a little tricky for you right now, the pattern being shown in the second diagram (in the key of C major, C-F-G progression). There are many patterns you can find similar to these on the fretboard, but these two are the most common. Seeking out these patterns through your knowledge of the notes on the neck will actually help you memorize them better.

As we said before, always use the correct shape for whichever string your root is on. If your root is on the low E, use the G or E shape. If your root is on the A, use the C or A shape. If your root is on the D, your D shape is the only option.

Practice switching between the shapes, building progressions with this formula, and changing keys each day for the next few weeks. Having these simple skills memorized will help you countless times in the future. Even if you don't want to write songs, you're going to need these skills at some point, whether it's to transpose a song you're learning, cover for yourself if you forget a part, or if you just end up wanting to jam with someone. These simple things are too often overlooked and usually end with players becoming overwhelmed, frustrated, and ultimately quitting. Take the time to learn everything, even if it seems simple or small. It all adds up over time and helps build your foundation while adding to your overall understanding of music.

Application

Now that you've learned all these bits of theory, moveable chords, and scale shapes, you need to know what to do with them. First off, practice your shapes every day. Don't memorize them for a week and then forget them! The biggest mistake guitarists make is not making a practice routine. It's so commonly overlooked, which is why most beginners, especially those self-taught, always seem to get frustrated at slow progress. Don't do what so many others do! Make a schedule for yourself, even if you only get the chance to practice a few hours a week, and always start with a warm-up.

Practice Routines

When putting together your practice routine, *always* start by warming up with the shapes you learned previously from the CAGED system. Practice each shape: chord-scale-chord-arpeggio every day. Spending a good 15 minutes each day will increase your finger speed and dexterity. Within a few weeks, you'll be a whole lot faster than you are today if you continuously practice them. And never forget: alternate your picking!

Metronomes tend to be an avoided subject for many guitarists, but having good timing is a very important skill that needs to be practiced as much as any other. If you're warming up with what you've learned and *are* using a metronome in your practice sessions, you're well on your way to becoming a great guitarist. Once you've warmed up well (and made sure you were in tune), start learning some songs. Don't just learn the easiest bit or only the first chord, pick a song you really want to know how to play (that's within your reach at the moment) and work on it. It will take practice to get it up to speed, and you will make mistakes, but with each song you learn you'll find yourself picking things up faster and faster.

Lastly, make sure to plan your session *before* you sit down to practice. Get a notebook and write down the night before what you need to review, what you want to learn, and what you're going to practice song-wise. Give yourself a good 15 minutes warming up with scales, chords, and little riffs to get your fingers moving. Afterwards, spend 15 minutes sight-reading music, then another 20 on theory and technique. Most importantly of all, practice the songs you want to learn to play. Don't overwhelm yourself trying to learn multiple pieces at once just take your time on one song and practice it each day. Learning the tough part of the song first will actually allow you to learn the song quicker. Keep that in mind if you ever want to learn a song with a hard solo or quick riff. Even if it's a chord change that you get stuck on, practice it. Don't leave out little details just because their tough or seem too small for people to realize, learning the song (or anything) correctly is key to sounding great when you play.

As you progress, you'll find yourself gaining speed and being able to play challenging things more easily if you spend the time practicing.

Techniques

Sustains & Shifts

Sustains are simply when you hold down a note and let it continue to ring out. Shifting is when you move your hand up or down the fretboard. For example, build any bar chord and then move it somewhere else on the neck, that's a shift!

Slides

Sliding into, out of, or to and fro a note is a simple but highly effective and cool sounding technique. If you read guitar tabs (as you should) slides are represented with a slash. As an example, fret the 5th fret of the A string and pick it. Keep pressure down so the note continues to sustain as you slide your finger to the 7th fret, that's a slide! In most cases, you shouldn't hit the second (landing) note with your pick; the pressure you keep on the string should make the note sustain the entire time.

Vibrato

Vibrato is the most expressive and emotional technique on the guitar. Play any note on your guitar neck and keep pressure down while you wiggle your finger up and down, back and forth, or in a circle. There's really no wrong way to do vibrato and the speed and direction of your vibrato will become part of your distinct playing style.

Putting vibrato on a note is the same as bending it back and forth multiple times in a row, meaning you can do a half-step vibrato (typically what you'll hear) or a wide vibrato, which usually spans a whole-step. If you were to hold down the 5th fret of the D string (giving you a G note) and did a half-step vibrato, you'd push the string upwards on the fretboard a half-step (G#) and then bring it back down to the starting note (G) you could then continue to pull it downwards to G# again, repeating this motion again and again (as quickly as you wanted to). This up and down vibrato technique can also span a whole-step (i.e. wide vibrato; you'd be going from a G to A note).

Bends

To bend, fret a note then push upwards (or downwards) to raise the fretted note's pitch. In most cases, you'll want to fret whatever note is going to be bent with your third finger so you can support it with your other two (first and second), then push up (e, B, G) or pull down (E, A, D) on the string to raise the pitch. When bending strings, don't just use your fingers, use your entire wrist. Anchor your thumb on the top of the guitar neck and keep your fingers locked in position. Your fingers shouldn't move, your wrist should be moving your fingers in order to bend the string.

Bending on an acoustic guitar is much tougher than it would be on an electric guitar. When you first start practicing bends, start with small ones to make sure you don't hurt your hands.

Hammer-ons

Hammering-on to a note is actually quite simple. Play any note then use another finger to hammer-on to that same string on another fret. Don't pick the string twice, just once on your starting note. The pressure of your finger landing on the string should make that note sound out. Your goal is to eventually have these two notes ring out at the same volume.

Pull-offs

These are the opposite of hammer-ons. Play any note while fretting another note "behind" it with another finger. Pick the string then pull off from the note with the tip of your finger so the other note you were fretting rings out. The pulling-off motion should be plucking the string, not just lifting off. Just like with hammer-ons, you eventually want both notes to ring out at the same volume.

Palm Mutes

Sometimes, songs will require you to have a muffled sound when playing. This is accomplished by palm muting. Fret a chord, then take the edge of your strumming hand's palm and lay it against all of the strings. Your hand should be near the bridge. When you strum, you should still be able to hear the chord, but the sound should be muffled; if you're unable to decipher the pitches of the strings when palm muting, you're muting too much and should move your hand back towards the bridge. There's no need to put any pressure down on the strings, just lay your hand lightly across them.

Chord Changes

While changing chords isn't exactly a technique, being a good acoustic guitarist requires good rhythm skills. The speed at which you're able to pick and strum along with how quickly you can change chords will determine your skill level. Practicing changing between chords quickly and smoothly will make playing songs and tough rhythms much easier. You should also practice string-skipping and string-switching with your strumming hand so that you're able to pick arpeggios easily.

Spend at least 10 minutes every day switching between chords, picking strings, and strumming tricky rhythms. Using a metronome will help you keep time. Tap your foot with the click and listen for it to make sure you aren't too fast or too slow. Playing slowly can actually be harder than playing fast, so practice playing at many different speeds.

On top of building and playing progressions of your own, being able to play songs by another musician will also help build your skills. While it's good to apply your own style to songs, being able to play exactly like the recorded track will also help improve your abilities. While it's good to pick a genre to focus on, as a guitarist, you need to be very versatile in what you can play. Whether its blues, rock, or country, being able to pick up your guitar and play the same chords in a dozen different styles should be one of the many things you strive to achieve. If you're looking for songs to learn, Tom Petty and Bob Dylan tunes are a good place to start.

CAGED System Application I

Now that we've learned some techniques, let's learn how to apply the CAGED system. Other than building up our speed and dexterity, the scales and arpeggios can be used to improvise over chords and compose solos.

Key	I	ii	iii	IV	V	vi	vii
C	C	D	E	F	G	A	B
D	D	E	F#	G	A	B	C#
E	E	F#	G#	A	B	C#	D#
F	F	G	A	Bb	C	D	E
G	G	A	B	C	D	E	F#
A	A	B	C#	D	E	F#	G#
B	B	C#	D#	E	F#	G#	A#

Chord-Scale-Key Connections

Say we have our I-IV-V progression again, in the key of C major, how can we use our scales to improvise over it? Let's say we have our chords C-F-G on loop. Here's what we need to do: we should know by now that these chords are obviously made up of notes, but we need to figure out which notes. Let's build our C chord on the A string then fill in the notes. All we're going to do is write in the notes that we're fretting within this shape, as shown. We'll do the same with our F and G chords.

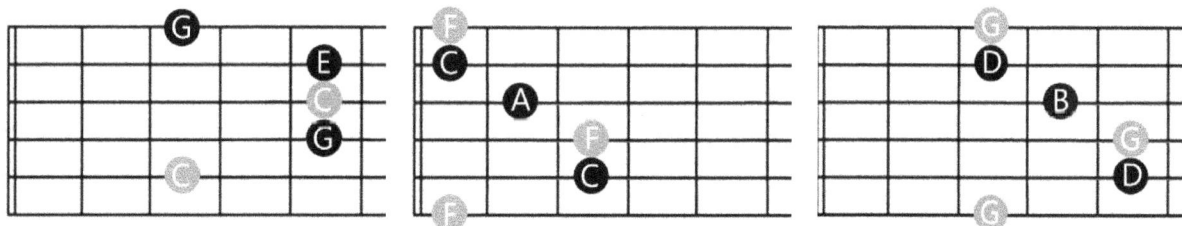

Looking again at major key chord chart above (same as on page 34), notice how the notes that make up each of these chords are the I, iii, and V notes from the chart (these are the same notes we use to build our arpeggios). All major chords follow this pattern. Since

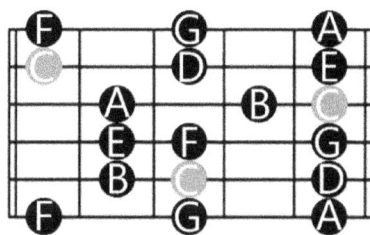

we're in the key of C major, let's take a look at our notes in the C major scale. Let's use the A shape since our C major chord is played as an A shape in this example. Our scale notes are: C-D-E-F-G-A-B. If you have a look at our chart at the top of the page, you'll see it matches up with the notes exactly. The chart shows us all of our notes in all of our major scales. No matter what

shape this scale was played as, all C major scales have these same notes. Now, let's see how the notes from our chords relate to these scale notes. If you take a moment, you'll notice all of these notes that make up the chords can be found within our C major scale, and they follow a pattern.

Chord Notes

C-D-**E**-F-**G**-A-B

C-D-E-**F**-G-**A**-B

C-**D**-E-F-**G**-A-**B**

To get the three notes for each chord, start on the root note, then pick every other note until you have three. For example, to get our C major chord notes, all we did was write out a C major scale (same notes you saw in the chart), and bolded our root note, C. Next, we'll skip a note then bold the 3rd note of the scale. Again, to get our final note, we'll skip one, then bold G. We can do the same for our F major chord notes. Bold our root F, skip one, bold A, and skip one more, go back to the beginning (it repeats) and bold C. For the final chord, G, we bold our root, skip one, bold B, skip one, and bold D.

Intervals

When we take a note, skip one, then take another one, we're going up in thirds. A third is a type of interval on the guitar, like a half-step or whole-step. In fact, a major third interval is the same as four half-steps and a minor third is 3 half-steps. This means we can count up from our starting note four notes (four half-steps) and get our major third interval. We can also count up three notes (three half-steps) from our starting note to get our minor third interval.

Up four notes from C is: C#, D, D#, then E! C to E is a major third interval.

Up three notes from E is: F-F#-G. E to G in a minor third interval.

You can find the notes for any major chord by using a major third then minor third interval. In our scale chart, going up a third is just skipping over one note (which is why the scale chart is so handy!). We'll get more into intervals another time, for now, you just need to know the proper theoretical term for what we're doing.

Soloing Over the I-IV-V

The I-IV-V progression is too popular to ignore, which is why we're going to practice soloing over it. The I chord always determines the key you're in, so if the I chord is C, you're in C major, if it's F, you're in F major. Let's stick with C major since we've been using it thus far. Our I-IV-V progression in C major is C-F-G. As we've seen before, all of the notes in all three of these chords can be found within our major scale. So, if you're in the key of C major, all notes from the C major scale can be used in your solo. Same goes for any other key, the corresponding major scale notes will work over a I-IV-V progression. Since we already know the CAGED scale and arpeggio shapes, we just need to shift them all into C major so we can use them. Once you have your shapes in the right key, you can use any of those shapes over all of the chords and sound fine. Of course, emphasizing certain notes can seem odd if a chord change happens, or you just hold a note a little too long. Don't make the mistake of blocking everything out; you need to hear what's going on. Play *with* the music, not on top of it.

Minor Pentatonic Shapes

A pentatonic scale is simply a scale made up of five notes, the minor pentatonic is what we're going to learn now and it's literally used in thousands of solos. It's moveable just like all other scale shapes we've learned, but here it's written in G minor (remember it's a minor scale shape), go ahead and play it:

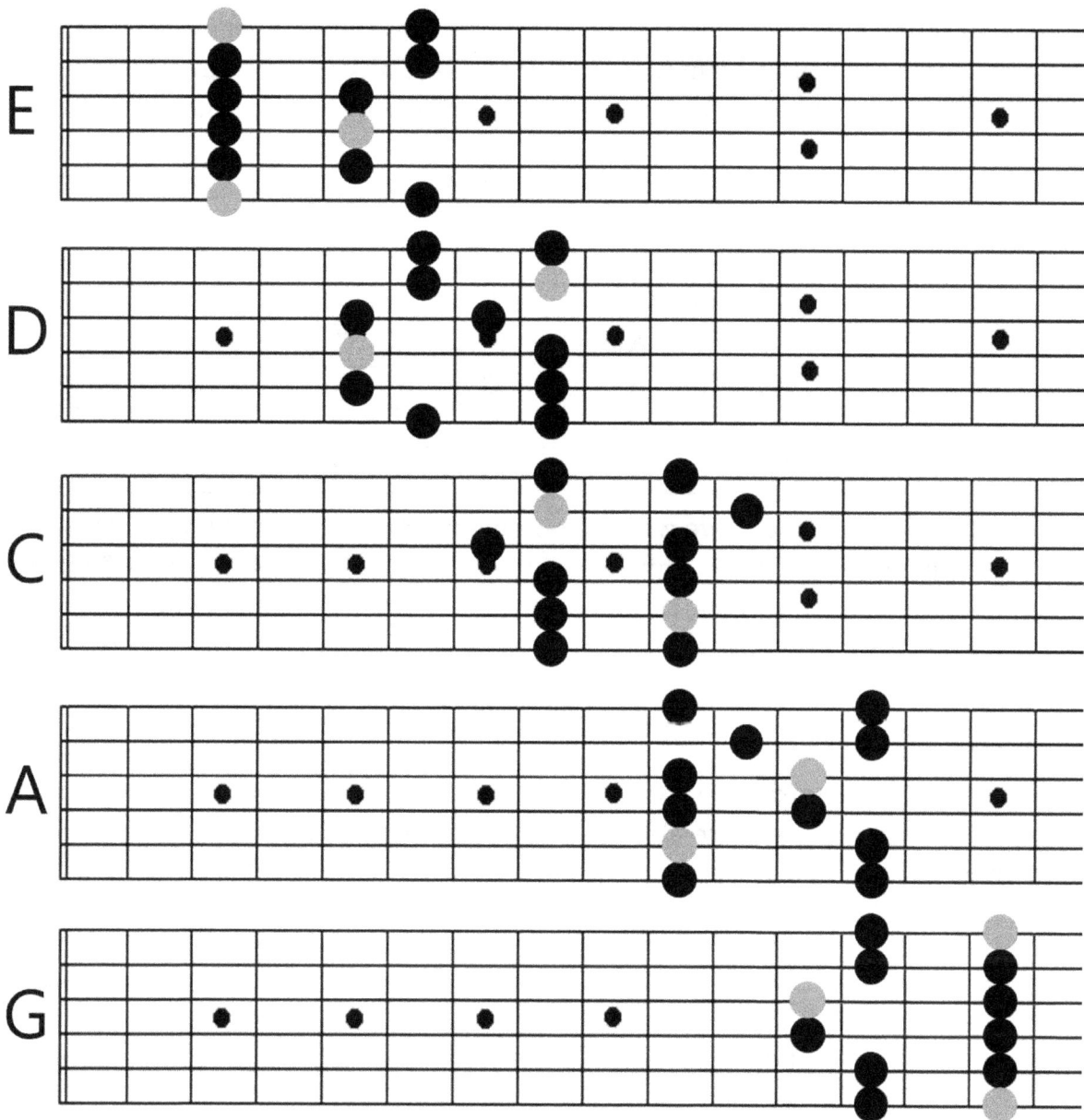

Play through these scales just like any other: start on the lowest (in pitch) root note, play all the way up to the end, then back down to the notes before the root you started on, and end by playing back up to your starting note. Memorize where these root notes are located within the shape. Putting some kind of accent on them like vibrato as you play through the scale will help your fingers and ears memorize their locations.

41

Relative Minor

While it's a concept normally reserved for guitarists getting deep into music theory, it's not really that hard of a concept to grasp. First, let's explain what it is. Every major key has a relative minor. Relative minor can be used in many instances, but most commonly when there is a major chord progression playing and you want to have a deeper, perhaps sadder tone to your guitar part. Playing the relative minor scale or a relative minor chord of a major key will sound fine because some notes will be shared between the major and relative minor keys (very important notes). To find the relative minor, grab your major key chord chart (same as we've seen before), and have a look at any key you want to play in:

Key	I	ii	iii	IV	V	vi	vii
C	C	D	E	F	G	A	B
D	D	E	F#	G	A	B	C#
E	E	F#	G#	A	B	C#	D#
F	F	G	A	Bb	C	D	E
G	G	A	B	C	D	E	F#
A	A	B	C#	D	E	F#	G#
B	B	C#	D#	E	F#	G#	A#

Let's say C major is our key and we want its relative minor. All we're going to do is take the sixth note, which happens to be A. This means the relative minor of C major is A minor. B minor is the relative minor of D major, and so forth. Just take the sixth note and that's your relative minor key.

Minor Key Chord Chart

Just like the major key chord chart exists, there's also one for minor keys, as shown below. It's important to note that there are also flat and sharp major and minor keys, but we included only the natural keys here for ease of reading. Complete charts are on page 46.

Key	i	ii	III	iv	v	VI	VII
Cm	C	D	Eb	F	G	Ab	Bb
Dm	D	E	F	G	A	Bb	C
Em	E	F#	G	A	B	C	D
Fm	F	G	Ab	Bb	C	Db	Eb
Gm	G	A	Bb	C	D	Eb	F
Am	A	B	C	D	E	F	G
Bm	B	C#	D	E	F#	G	A

Lowercase numerals should be played as minor and uppercase should be played as major. In minor keys, ii is actually diminished (we'll learn some moveable diminished chord shapes a little later in this book).

CAGED System Application II

Now that you know your minor pentatonic shapes and the minor keys, we can add in more possibilities for soloing and improvising over chord progressions. Since we know that over our I-IV-V progression in C major we can play any of the scale or arpeggio shapes (in the key of C major), we can also now use the minor pentatonic scale shapes. Since the pentatonic shapes are minor, we need to use the relative minor of C major. Remember, we just take the sixth note and that's our relative minor key, making A minor the relative minor of C major.

Now, you just have to move your minor pentatonic shapes into the key of A minor (just move all the roots to an A note, and keep them in order). Now we can also use those pentatonic shapes in our solo.

Let's review: if we have our I-IV-V progression in C major, then our chords are C-F-G. We can use all of the CAGED shapes in the key of C major to solo over these chords. We can also apply our knowledge of relative minor keys and use our minor pentatonic scale shapes in the key of A minor to solo over the chords, too.

Adding Chord Notes

If we were to write out all of the notes played within each pentatonic scale shape in the key of A minor, it'd take a lot of time. Recall that the chord charts seen previously have all of the notes for all major and minor scales. Our pentatonic scales only use five of these notes; the minor pentatonic scales follow the formula of 1-b3-4-5-b7. This means we just take our 1st, 3rd, 4th, 5th, and 7th notes from any *major* key and write them out. In A major, those notes are: A-C#-D-E-G#. Now, in the formula it showed b3 and b7. This just means that we need to flat these two notes, or lower them by 1-half step (1 fret wire). That gives us our A minor pentatonic notes: A-C-D-E-G.

If we go back to our progression yet again, C-F-G, we can think about the three notes in each of those chords. You'll find that they're all part of our A minor pentatonic scale, except for F and B. If we're using our minor pentatonic scale over these chords, we can add these two notes into our solo, even though they aren't included in the shapes. We would do this to make the chords sound like they "fit in" better with our solo.

Recap & Review

It's easy enough to do all of these things with any key. Just get your major progression down and write it out. Get the notes from each of these chords and write them out, too (all together would be helpful so you don't have to deal with repeating notes). Move your CAGED shapes into the right key and use them, and/or find the relative minor of the key (it's just the sixth note) and move your minor pentatonic shapes over. You can leave it at that, or add in the missing chord notes by writing out your pentatonic scale notes and adding in whichever ones are missing from the list.

Scale Formulas

All scales, whether major, minor, or pentatonic, follow an intervallic formula. This simply means each note is a certain distance apart from the next, no matter the key. This is why all scales of the same kind sound somewhat similar, like C major will sound similar to B major because even though the notes are different, they're all the same distance apart from one another within each scale.

Basic Formulas

The major formula is W-W-H-W-W-W-H. Start on any note, then go up a whole step in the musical alphabet, then another whole-step, then a half-step, and so forth. If you did it with C major, you'd get C-D-E-F-G-A-B-C. Notice these notes match up with what's shown in the charts you've seen before. These charts are showing you the notes in all of the scales. Memorizing your scale formulas will come in handy time and time again.

The minor scale formula is: W-H-W-W-H-W-W.

The minor pentatonic scale formula is: 1-b3-4-5-b7. Use this formula in any major key to get the corresponding minor pentatonic notes. For instance, we'd use this formula in the key of A major to get our A minor pentatonic notes.

Alternate Formulas

All scales are based upon the major scale. In music there is almost always more than one way of going about something. For instance, instead of using these intervallic formulas like W-W-H-W-W-W-H we can take our major scale and use numeric formulas instead (like the one for the minor pentatonic scale). We'll just take certain notes and flat or sharp them to get a scale.

Parallel/Natural Minor

Another way to get the minor scale is simply to take our major key notes and flat the 3rd, 6th and 7th notes. This is exactly what we did to get from our major key chord chart to the minor key chord chart. This is the same as using our minor intervallic formula as shown above. Both should be memorized, but this one tends to be easier to use in most cases. There are in fact multiple minor scales. This particular minor scale is known as the "parallel" minor because we have the same root as the major scale (like G major and G minor) but we follow a slightly different formula.

To get the parallel minor of G major, we just take the G major notes: G-A-B-C-D-E-F#-G, then flat the 3rd, 6th and 7th, giving us: G-A-Bb-C-D-Eb-F-G.

Parallel and natural minor are the same thing, but the term parallel is used to show that a minor scale is parallel (or related) to a major scale in that they share the same root note. In the following breakdown chart, natural and parallel minor are separated for easy reference, but they are the same scale and therefore both follow the exact same formulas.

Harmonic Minor

The harmonic minor scale can be found by following the formula: W-H-W-W-H-W-H. You can also get the harmonic minor scale by taking the major key notes then flattening the 3rd and 6th notes. The harmonic minor of G major (or G harmonic minor) is: G-A-Bb-C-D-Eb-F#-G.

Melodic Minor

The formula for the melodic minor scale is W-H-W-W-W-W-H. It can also be found by taking the major key notes and flattening the 3rd note.

The melodic minor of G major (or G melodic minor) is: G-A-Bb-C-D-E-F#-G.

Relative Minor

Remember, to find the relative minor just take the 6th note of any major key/scale.

You may notice that C major and A minor are the *only* two scales that do not contain sharp or flat notes. This is specific to these two keys/scales. Knowing this will also help you realize that any major key and its relative minor key contain the same notes in the same order, you just start somewhere different.

For example, the C major scale is C-D-E-F-G-A-B which repeats again and again, while the A minor scale is A-B-C-D-E-F-G. If you take the C major scale and start on the 6th note (to get the relative minor) you'll get the A minor scale exactly as you would if you used the formula for parallel/natural minor. So, all we're doing is taking a major scale and starting on a different note (the 6th) to get our relative minor notes.

Breakdown Chart

This breakdown chart is a handy thing to keep around, but having the formulas memorized will be even more helpful. Practice writing out each scale in different keys and eventually it will become second nature. Have a look at the examples in the key of G to make sure you're doing everything correctly.

Scale Name	Formula (From Scratch)	Formula Based on Major Key/Scale	Example
Major	W-W-H-W-W-W-H	1-2-3-4-5-6-7	G-A-B-C-D-E-F#
Natural m.	W-H-W-W-H-W-W	1-2-b3-4-5-b6-b7	G-A-Bb-C-D-Eb-F
Parallel m.	W-H-W-W-H-W-W	1-2-b3-4-5-b6-b7	G-A-Bb-C-D-Eb-F
Harmonic m.	W-H-W-W-H-W-H	1-2-b3-4-5-b6-7	G-A-Bb-C-D-Eb-F#
Melodic m.	W-H-W-W-W-W-H	1-2-b3-4-5-6-7	G-A-Bb-C-D-E-F#
Pentatonic m.	Use Other Formula	1-b3-4-5-b7	G-Bb-C-D-F

Now is the time to realize that corresponding keys and scales share the same notes (so the G major scale and the key of G major both contain the notes G-A-B-C-D-E-F#). So, if someone talks about the notes in a major key they're also referring to the notes in the major scale (and vice versa).

Major & Minor Key Chord Charts

Here are the complete chord charts for all major keys:

Key	I	ii	iii	IV	V	vi	vii
C	C	D	E	F	G	A	B
F	F	G	A	Bb	C	D	E
Bb	Bb	C	D	Eb	F	G	A
Eb	Eb	F	G	Ab	Bb	C	D
Ab	Ab	Bb	C	Db	Eb	F	G
Db	Db	Eb	F	Gb	Ab	Bb	C
Gb	Gb	Ab	Bb	Cb	Db	Eb	F
B	B	C#	D#	E	F#	G#	A#
E	E	F#	G#	A	B	C#	D#
A	A	B	C#	D	E	F#	G#
D	D	E	F#	G	A	B	C#
G	G	A	B	C	D	E	F#

The minor key chord chart is as follows:

Key	i	ii	III	iv	v	VI	VII
C	C	D	Eb	F	G	Ab	Bb
F	F	G	Ab	Bb	C	Db	Eb
A#	A#	B#	C#	D#	E#	F#	G#
D#	D#	E#	F#	G#	A#	B	C#
G#	G#	A#	B	C#	D#	E	F#
C#	C#	D#	E	F#	G#	A	B
F#	F#	G#	A	B	C#	D	E
B	B	C#	D	E	F#	G	A
E	E	F#	G	A	B	C	D
A	A	B	C	D	E	F	G
D	D	E	F	G	A	Bb	C
G	G	A	Bb	C	D	Eb	F

Always remember that there needs to be one of each note in every key, so none should repeat. This is why we use both sharps and flats in theory. Notice that in the key of B major, we use F# not Gb. If we used Gb it wouldn't be written correctly, we need to have one of each note in each key, so we use F# instead.

Interval Breakdown

Interval Name	Fret Wires	Half-steps	Whole-steps	Degree Name
Unison	0	0	0	Root or Tonic
Minor Second	1	1	½	Flat Second
Major Second	2	2	1	Second
Minor Third	3	3	1 ½	Flat Third
Major Third	4	4	2	Third
Perfect Fourth	5	5	2 ½	Fourth
Diminished Fifth	6	6	3	Flat Fifth
Perfect Fifth	7	7	3 ½	Fifth
Augmented Fifth	8	8	4	Sharp Fifth
Major Sixth	9	9	4 ½	Sixth
Minor/Dom. 7th	10	10	5	Flat 7th
Major Seventh	11	11	5 ½	Seventh
Perfect Octave	12	12	6	First Octave

There are more interval types then these, but these are the intervals known as "simple intervals." Above them are "compound intervals" which we'll get into in book 2. The interval name is how we'll be referring to them, but we've included the degree name for reference. Within any scale there is something called "scale degrees" which are names and numbers for each note. The scale degrees were not included, but the degree names will give them to you. For example, the degree name for a minor second is "flat second." The scale degree of a flat second is "b2" which should look familiar. We use scale degrees in our formulas as you've seen before (now you know what they're called).

Memorizing the intervals is a big task, but one you should consider taking on as it's good to have these things memorized for reference. On a single string, practice playing different notes and quizzing yourself on the interval type. Don't just count the fret wires, know which notes you're playing and be able to work through the alphabet in your head to figure out the interval.

Ear-Training

Ear-training is when you learn to recognize different notes just by hearing them. There are two types of pitches people are said to have: perfect and relative. Perfect pitch is something people are believed to be born with, and not many people have it. They just seem to have a very good ear that can pick up the different pitches and recognize them.

If you don't have perfect pitch, you're with the rest of us who have to develop something called "relative pitch." It's called relative pitch because we learn and memorize the pitches by relating them to another note we know, which is when intervals come in. Intervals help you memorize notes by taking a root then playing another note a third or fifth (etc.) up from that note so your brain not only relates them to each other, but can start to memorize the names and locations of these pitches on the guitar.

Chord Construction

Triads

Before, we briefly discussed how our chords were constructed using three notes. More specifically, you take the root of the chord (the chord name) go to that key, then take the 1st, 3rd and 5th notes to build the chord. Chords that use only three notes are known as triads. Each note in a triad is given a name, known as the root, third or fifth. These are the degree names. The third is either a minor or major third above the root note. The fifth is a minor or major third above the third, it's also a diminished, perfect, or augmented fifth above the root note (hence its name).

Major Triads

Major triads contain a major third and perfect fifth interval. Now would be the time to note that perfect intervals are neither major nor minor. The written formula for a major triad is R-3-5 which is using the scale degrees. It may also appear as 0-4-7, showing you the amount of half-steps.

Another way to describe their construction would be to say it's a major third with a minor third stacked on top of it. For example, a C major triad would have the notes C-E-G. C to E is a major third and E to G is a minor third.

Minor Triads

Minor triads have a minor third and perfect fifth interval and are written as either R-b3-5 or 0-3-7. Alternatively, you could say it's a minor third with a major third stacked above it. An A minor triad, for example, would contain A to C (minor third) and C to E (major third).

Diminished Triads

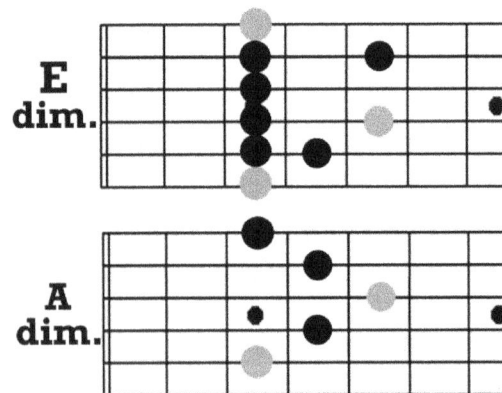

You may remember that some notes in the major and minor scales were to be played as diminished chords. Diminished triads are made with a minor third and diminished fifth interval, represented by R-b3-b5 or 0-3-6. You could also say it's built by stacking two minor thirds on top of one another. Shown are two moveable diminished chord shapes with their roots on the E and A strings. Practice these shapes so you can use other progressions that include diminished chords.

Augmented Triads

Augmented triads are built using a major third and augmented fifth interval. This can be shown with R-3-#5 or 0-4-8. You can also say that they're built using two major thirds stacked on top of one-another. Augmented chords are also called augmented fifth chords because the 5th note is augmented.

Octave Shapes

Knowing how to quickly find matching pairs of notes will help a lot when playing songs. Octave shapes take any note then find a matching note that's one octave higher. Remember, an octave is 8 whole-steps or 12 half-steps. The open string note and corresponding 12th fret note is an example of an octave.

Here are four of the octave shapes:

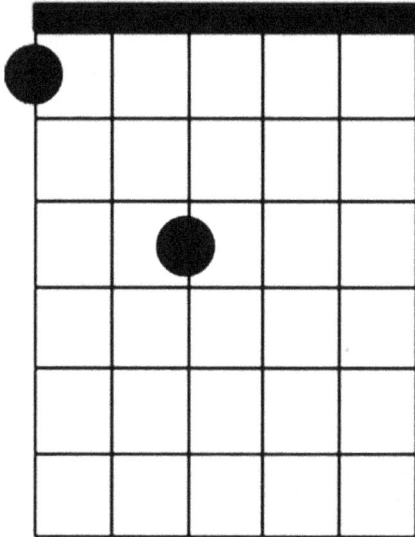

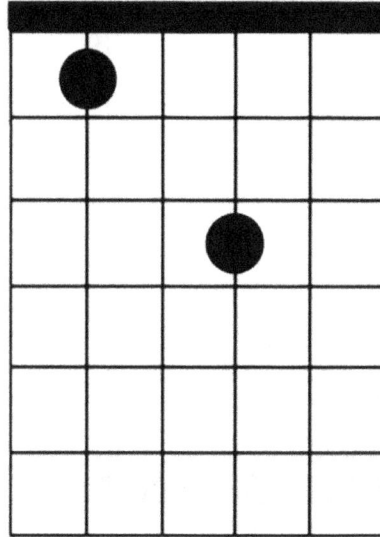

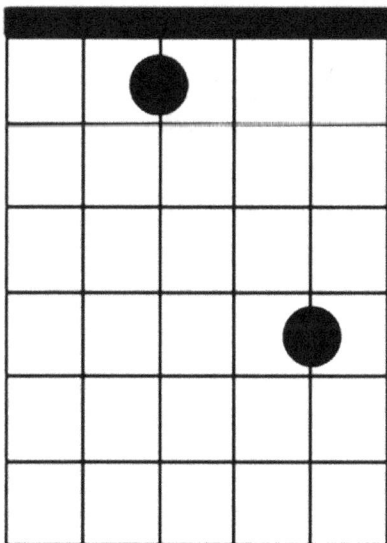

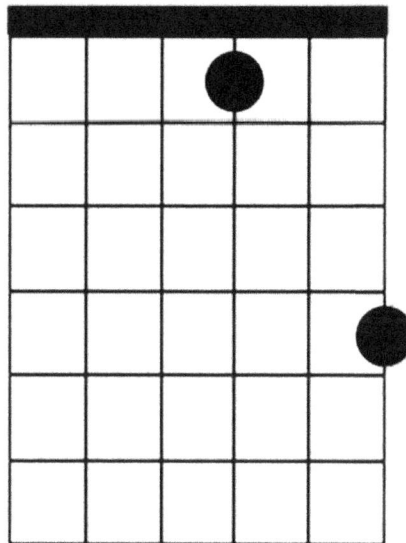

Take a moment to memorize these shapes and you'll be able to quickly find root notes for scale shapes, chords, and arpeggios. Some of these shapes may look familiar to you because your scale shapes have root notes that follow these same patterns. In fact, these octave shapes are taken from the CAGED scale shapes. Just find two of the gray notes in any of the CAGED scale diagrams and you'll get these same shapes (you'll also find an additional shape with the root on the A string for you to use).

Power/Fifth Chords

Now that you know your intervals and octave shapes, we can learn how to play power chords. These are moveable two and three note chords that usually have their root on the E or A string. Here are the four most common power chord shapes:

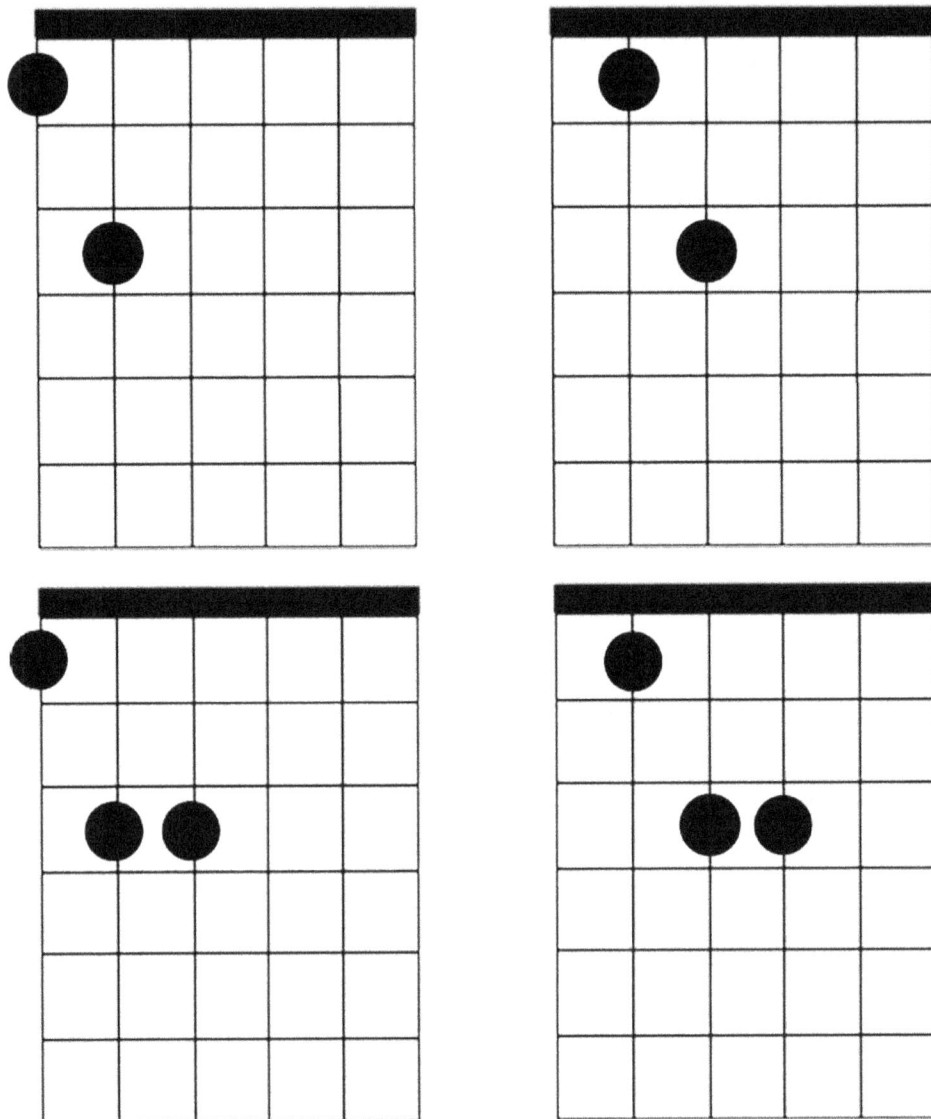

The shapes on the top are using only a perfect fifth interval. Remember this type of interval is neither major nor minor, meaning our power chords aren't either. This is one of the reasons why they're referred to as power chords, but they're properly called 5th chords because of the interval they use. Wherever your root note is will determine your chord. With the E shape in the first fret you'll have an F power chord, or an F5 chord as it's properly known. The bottom shapes tend to sound fuller because they're adding in another root note (you can see it's just the octave shape with the added fifth interval in between). Both shapes are common, but the three-note power chord tends to be preferred.

Alternate Tunings

Your guitar should stay in standard tuning for the majority of the time so you can practice all of these scales and chords correctly, but there will be times when changing the tuning will be helpful. Alternate tunings include open and dropped tunings. Here's a breakdown of some common ones.

Standard	E1	A1	D2	G2	B2	E3
Open C	C1	G1	C2	G2	C3	E3
Open A	E1	A1	C#2	E2	A2	E3
Open G	D1	G1	D2	G2	B2	D3
Open E	E1	B1	E2	G#2	B2	E3
Open D	D1	A1	D2	F#2	A2	D3
Drop C	C1	G1	C2	G2	C3	E3
Drop A	A0	E1	A1	D2	F#2	B2
Drop D	D1	A1	D2	G2	B2	E3

There are many alternate tunings out there, but drop D seems to be the most common. When you tune your guitar to another tuning, you have to use different chord shapes as the ones you've learned before will no longer apply.

The numbers behind the note names are showing you the pitch of the note. On staff, you already know where the first-position notes appear so you have these as reference. The higher the number, the higher it should be placed on the staff and therefore the higher in pitch. Here's a quick overview of the notes:

If you're stuck on where to find these notes on your guitar, find the open note pitches in standard tuning and use them as reference (E1-A1-D2-G2-B2-E3).

Song & Scale Book

Skip, Skip

Jingle Rock

When the Saints Go Marching In

Since this starts with a rest, you could also write it as a pickup rhythm.

Yankee Doodle

Scarborough Fair

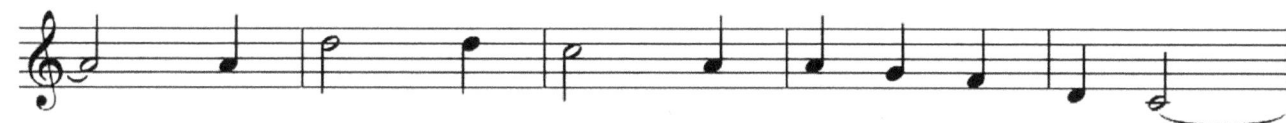

Sailor's Rock

Rockin' Riff

Open Major Scales

Here are the CAGED major scales in open-position. Write out the other major scales on your own to help you memorize note locations.

Here's some blank staff to write in other scales:

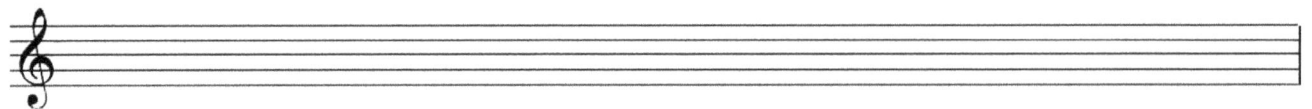

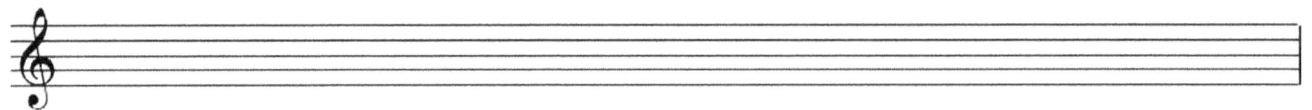

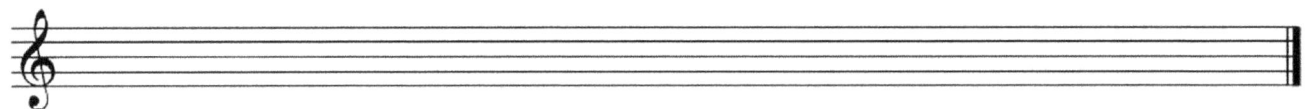

Moving On

Before you go, here are five things to never forget for as long as you play guitar:

1. Review Everything You've Learned Multiple Times
2. Plan Your Sessions
3. Practice Regularly
4. Use a Metronome
5. And Have Fun!

Number five is perhaps the most important tip of all. Whether you're tuning your guitar or just changing the strings, have fun doing it; life's just too short not to.

Since you've now completed this book, let's review everything you now know:

- The Musical Alphabet
- Standard & Alternate Tunings
- How to Read Tab & Musical Notation
- How to Do a Bunch of Cool Techniques
- Open-Position Chords & Scales
- Moveable Shapes and the Entire CAGED Major System
- How to Build Chord Progressions in Any Major Key
- Intervals & How Chords are Constructed
- Octave Shapes
- Power Chords

And so much more! You need to review this stuff regularly of course, and remember you can never practice too much. If you want more topics, techniques, and theory studies, check out book 2, which includes:

- Advanced Techniques
- The CAGED Minor System
- Circle of Fifths Studies
- More Sight-Reading Practice
- An In-depth Look Into Scale Modes
- Scale Harmonization
- More on Chord Construction
- More Moveable Chord Shapes to Use

And of course a lot more! In the meantime, check out LutzAcademy.com where you'll find free resources for your playing, like blank tabs, diagrams and more.

Now go practice!

9 780692 319512